HAYEK
FOR THE 21ST CENTURY

The Mises Institute dedicates this volume to the US Justice Charitable Foundation Inc. for its generous support and sponsorship.

HAYEK

FOR THE 21ST CENTURY

ESSAYS IN POLITICAL ECONOMY

EDITED BY
THOMAS J. DILORENZO

MISESINSTITUTE
AUBURN, ALABAMA

The Mises Institute is a nonprofit organization that exists to promote teaching and research in the Austrian School of economics, individual freedom, honest history, and international peace, in the tradition of Ludwig von Mises and Murray N. Rothbard.

Nonpolitical, nonpartisan, and non-PC, we advocate a radical shift in the intellectual climate, away from statism and toward a private property order. We believe that our foundational ideas are of permanent value, and oppose all efforts at compromise, sellout, and amalgamation of these ideas with fashionable political, cultural, and social doctrines inimical to their spirit.

The Mises Institute is funded entirely by voluntary contributions from individuals, businesses, and foundations. We do not accept any government money.

For more information, visit mises.org, email us at contact@mises.org, or call 1.800.OF.MISES.

Special thanks is extended to the Estate of F. A. Hayek for permission to reproduce "Why the Worst Get on Top" and "The Meaning of Competition." Thanks is also given to Dr. Bruce Caldwell, the executor of the F. A. Hayek estate, for his assistance.

In addition, thanks is also extended to the *American Economic Review*, the University of Chicago Press, *The University of Chicago Law Review*, *Southern Economic Journal*, the Nobel Foundation, and the Institute for Economic Affairs for permission to reproduce the essays included in this volume.

Published 2025 by the Mises Institute

Mises Institute
518 W. Magnolia Ave.
Auburn, AL 36832
mises.org
contact@mises.org

ISBN: 978-1-61016-790-1

Contents

Contents

Introduction

In a February 7, 2000, article in *The New Yorker*, journalist John Cassidy wrote that "it is hardly an exaggeration to refer to the twentieth century as the Hayek century." He said this because of Friedrich Hayek's prominent role throughout the century in defending free market capitalism and his critiques of socialism, especially his writings on the importance of decentralized knowledge in economic decision-making. Hayek lived to see his ideas proven correct with the worldwide collapse of socialism in the late eighties and early nineties. Watching the images of the collapse on television he said to his son, "I told you so."

The Knowledge Problem

The "knowledge problem" is Hayek's key contribution to the critique of socialism. It recognizes the commonsense notion that what makes the economic world go around is the use of knowledge by all kinds of people with different abilities, educations, experiences, and skills. Thanks to this international division of labor *and knowledge*, we collaborate "as though led by an invisible hand" in order to mutually prosper. It all depends of course on freedom—the freedom to own property, to pursue a profession of your choosing, to start and run a business, to buy and sell, to be guided in your decisions by free market prices.

By contrast, socialism in all of its varieties is based on the opposite idea—that what is supposedly needed for prosperity is totalitarian powers in the hands of a small number of politicians and "planners" who will forcefully impose a single plan on an entire society. Hayek labeled this "the fatal conceit" of socialism in his last book. The entire world now knows that he was right, and all of the socialist tyrants and their propagandists and court historians were (and are) wrong.

Hayek's "The Use of Knowledge in Society" and "The Pretense of Knowledge," reprinted here, are the two best expositions of the Hayekian knowledge problem. Indeed, John Cassidy credited Hayek with providing an explanation of the workings of "the information age" of the internet that would develop some fifty years after he first started writing about the importance of decentralized information in society. This is not mere speculation on Cassidy's part. As just one example, the cofounder of Wikipedia, Jimmy Wales, claims to have gotten the idea for Wikipedia as an Auburn University undergraduate finance student after Mises Institute Research Fellow Mark Thornton got him to read "The Use of Knowledge in Society." Hayek called free market capitalism guided by private property and free market prices a "telecommunications system," which Cassidy suggested was "one of the great insights of the [twentieth] century."

Hayek's Demolition of Socialists and Their Ideas

Hayek wrote in a 1961 *Southern Economic Journal* article ("The *Non Sequitur* of the 'Dependence Effect,'" republished here) that for over a hundred years socialists had argued that "the problem of production" had been solved, so that "only the problem of distribution remains." At the time, the "latest form of this old contention" was in the form of numerous books by the socialist Harvard economist John Kenneth Galbraith, the best known of which was *The Affluent Society*. Galbraith argued in books and articles that all "essential needs" are already met, and that most of what people think are other "needs" are really fake needs created by the brainwashing effects of advertising. Only "innate" needs that we think of ourselves are useful, said Galbraith; everything else that is brought to our attention by others is therefore useless and wasteful. Therefore, the argument went, government should tax more and spend more for what *it* deems to be our *genuinely* useful needs. What is genuinely useful would of course be determined by politicians—presumably with the assistance of John Kenneth Galbraith.

Hayek called this argument "a complete *non sequitur*." It implies for one thing that "the whole cultural achievement of man is not important." The only genuinely innate human needs, said Hayek, are food, shelter, and sex. Everything else is brought to our attention by someone. Hayek's article is a complete demolition of the Galbraithian system and his life's work of promoting what Hayek called increasing "the share of the resources whose use is determined by political authority and the coercion of any dissenting minority."

In 1949 Hayek authored "The Intellectuals and Socialism" in *The University of Chicago Law Review*. His argument is as relevant today as it was then—if not *more* relevant. Contrary to the common argument that "intellectuals" have little influence on day-to-day discussions about public policy, Hayek argued that "over somewhat longer periods they have probably never exercised so great an influence as they do today." He pointed out that socialism was never a "working class" movement but was always hatched from the utopian dreams of "theorists" who spent decades preaching their socialist utopianism in university classrooms and all throughout the culture. In many countries the result of this decades-long propagandizing for socialism was that the views held by socialist intellectuals became "the governing force of politics," wrote Hayek. The "intellectual" spreaders of socialist ideas were not just academics but also "journalists, teachers, ministers, lecturers, publicists, radio commentators, writers of fiction, cartoonists, and artists," among many others, including "scientists and doctors." It is "the intellectuals in this sense who decide what views and opinions are to reach us."

Eventually, so many institutions are taken over by socialists that an intellectual who espouses the philosophical foundations of a free society, by contrast, "soon discovers that it is unsafe to associate too closely with those who seem to share most of his convictions and he is driven into isolation." This sounds like a perfect description of today's American university world. Nevertheless, all is not lost, Hayek concluded. What is needed is education about a classical "liberal Utopia" to counter the endless promises of socialist utopias—not a "diluted kind of socialism," he wrote, but a "truly liberal radicalism" that does not pull punches to please any special interest group. Leave the compromising to the politicians, he advised.

Hayek was relentless in his devastating critiques of socialism and interventionism, and nowhere is this more on display than in his essay "The Meaning of Competition." By the 1940s the academic economics profession had adopted a straw-man argument version of competition. Rather than the Austrian School conception of competition as a dynamic, rivalrous discovery process, competition was newly defined as a static situation where "many" business firms all produced a homogeneous product and charged identical prices in a world where all market participants had "perfect knowledge" of everything—what consumers wanted, how to minimize costs and maximize profits, and so on. They called it "perfect competition." In his essay Hayek explained that "'perfect' competition means indeed the absence of all competitive activities" because all of it—product differentiation, price cutting, mergers, advertising—was all assumed away by the perfect competition "model."

This method of analysis was later labeled a "nirvana fallacy" by UCLA economist Harold Demsetz. Positing a utopian never-never land and comparing it to the real world, and then condemning real-world markets as "failed" because they are "imperfect," is one of the biggest hoaxes ever perpetrated by the economics profession.

In "Choice in Currency" Hayek did not oppose government issuance of money but instead opposed governmental monopoly and governments' "power to *limit* the kinds of money in which contracts may be concluded." Competing currencies could be valued "in seconds" with "electronic calculators," Hayek wrote, long before the invention of the cell phone. Competition in currencies would be the path to honest money, for "even the slightest deviation from the path of honesty would reduce the demand for their product." It is little wonder that Hayek's writings on competing currencies have become enormously popular among advocates of cryptocurrencies.

Hayekian Political Philosophy

Oddly enough, despite all of his contributions to economic science and his Nobel Prize, what Friedrich Hayek is most known for among the general public is his writings on political philosophy, in particular his infamous book *The Road to Serfdom*, a critique of collectivism in all its forms. Hayek did not distinguish between fascism and socialism, the former being just a variant of the latter, with a common hatred of private property, free enterprise, economic freedom in general, constitutionalism, and the rule of law. The most famous chapter of *The Road to Serfdom* is chapter 10, "Why the Worst Get on Top," republished here. Since any kind of socialism requires a central plan for all of society, it also requires the use of massive governmental force (and censorship of critics) to implement the plan. Consequently, the kind of people who would rise to the top of such a system are those with the fewest qualms about coercing, imprisoning, and brutalizing (or worse) their fellow citizens, wrote Hayek. That is why, he wrote, "the practice of socialism is everywhere totalitarian."

Hopefully, this brief introduction has helped the reader to understand why the journalist John Cassidy was so inspired by the power of Hayek's scholarship and writings that he made a case that the entire twentieth century (the good parts of it, anyway) should be thought of as "the Hayek century." Ludwig von Mises was surely right when, he said that "Doctor Hayek . . . will be remembered as one of the great economists" of all time.

Thomas J. DiLorenzo

CHAPTER 1

The Intellectuals and Socialism*

I

In all democratic countries, in the United States even more than elsewhere, a strong belief prevails that the influence of the intellectuals on politics is negligible. This is no doubt true of the power of intellectuals to make their peculiar opinions of the moment influence decisions, of the extent to which they can sway the popular vote on questions on which they differ from the current views of the masses. Yet over somewhat longer periods they have probably never exercised so great an influence as they do today in those countries. This power they wield by shaping public opinion.

In the light of recent history it is somewhat curious that this decisive power of the professional secondhand dealers in ideas should not yet be more generally recognized. The political development of the Western world during the last hundred years furnishes the clearest demonstration. Socialism has never and nowhere been at first a working class movement. It is by no means an obvious remedy for the obvious evil which the interests of that

*This text is based on the version of this essay published in *The University of Chicago Law Review* 16, no. 3 (1949): 417–33.

class will necessarily demand. It is a construction of theorists, deriving from certain tendencies of abstract thought with which for a long time only the intellectuals were familiar; and it required long efforts by the intellectuals before the working classes could be persuaded to adopt it as their program.

In every country that has moved toward socialism the phase of the development in which socialism becomes a determining influence on politics has been preceded for many years by a period during which socialist ideals governed the thinking of the more active intellectuals. In Germany this stage had been reached toward the end of the last century; in England and France, about the time of the First World War. To the casual observer it would seem as if the United States had reached this phase after World War II and that the attraction of a planned and directed economic system is now as strong among the American intellectuals as it ever was among their German or English fellows. Experience suggests that once this phase has been reached it is merely a question of time until the views now held by the intellectuals become the governing force of politics.

The character of the process by which the views of the intellectuals influence the politics of tomorrow is therefore of much more than academic interest. Whether we merely wish to foresee or attempt to influence the course of events, it is a factor of much greater importance than is generally understood. What to the contemporary observer appears as the battle of conflicting interests has indeed often been decided long before in a clash of ideas confined to narrow circles. Paradoxically enough, however, in general only the parties of the Left have done most to spread the belief that it was the numerical strength of the opposing material interests which decided political issues, whereas in practice these same parties have regularly and successfully acted as if they understood the key position of the intellectuals. Whether by design or driven by the force of circumstances, they have always directed their main effort toward gaining the support of this "elite," while the more conservative groups have acted, as regularly but unsuccessfully, on a more naive view of mass democracy and have usually vainly tried directly to reach and to persuade the individual voter.

II

The term intellectuals, however, does not at once convey a true picture of the large class to which we refer, and the fact that we have no better name by which to describe what we have called the secondhand dealers in ideas is not the least of the reasons why their power is not understood. Even persons who use the word intellectual mainly as a term of abuse are still inclined to withhold it from many who undoubtedly perform that characteristic function. This is neither that of the original thinker nor that of the scholar or expert in a particular field of thought. The typical intellectual need be neither: he need not possess special knowledge of anything in particular, nor need he even be particularly intelligent, to perform his role as intermediary in the spreading of ideas. What qualifies him for his job is the wide range of subjects on which he can readily talk and write, and a position or habits through which he becomes acquainted with new ideas sooner than those to whom he addresses himself.

Until one begins to list all the professions and activities which belong to the class, it is difficult to realize how numerous it is, how the scope for its activities constantly increases in modern society, and how dependent on it we all have become. The class does not consist only of journalists, teachers, ministers, lecturers, publicists, radio commentators, writers of fiction, cartoonists, and artists—all of whom may be masters of the technique of conveying ideas but are usually amateurs so far as the substance of what they convey is concerned. The class also includes many professional men and technicians, such as scientists and doctors, who through their habitual intercourse with the printed word become carriers of new ideas outside their own fields and who, because of their expert knowledge of their own subjects, are listened to with respect on most others. There is little that the ordinary man of today learns about events or ideas except through the medium of this class; and outside our special fields of work we are in this respect almost all ordinary men, dependent for our information and instruction on those who make it their job to keep abreast of opinion. It is the intellectuals in this sense who decide what views and opinions are to reach us, which facts are important enough to be told to us, and in what form and from what angle they are to be presented. Whether we shall ever learn of the results of the work of the expert and the original thinker depends mainly on their decision.

The layman, perhaps, is not fully aware to what extent even the popular reputations of scientists and scholars are made by that class and are inevitably affected by its views on subjects which have little to do with the merits of the real achievements. And it is specially significant for our problem that every scholar can probably name several instances from his field of men who have undeservedly achieved a popular reputation as great scientists solely because they hold what the intellectuals regard as "progressive" political views; but I have yet to come across a single instance where such a scientific pseudo-reputation has been bestowed for political reason on a scholar of more conservative leanings. This creation of reputations by the intellectuals is particularly important in the fields where the results of expert studies are not used by other specialists but depend on the political decision of the public at large. There is indeed scarcely a better illustration of this than the attitude which professional economists have taken to the growth of such doctrines as socialism or protectionism. There was probably at no time a majority of economists, who were recognized as such by their peers, favorable to socialism (or, for that matter, to protection). In all probability it is even true to say that no other similar group of students contains so high a proportion of its members decidedly opposed to socialism (or protection). This is the more significant as in recent times it is as likely as not that it was an early interest in socialist schemes for reform which led a man to choose economics for his profession. Yet it is not the predominant views of the experts but the views of a minority, mostly of rather doubtful standing in their profession, which are taken up and spread by the intellectuals.

The all-pervasive influence of the intellectuals in contemporary society is still further strengthened by the growing importance of "organization." It is a common but probably mistaken belief that the increase of organization increases the influence of the expert or specialist. This may be true of the expert administrator and organizer, if there are such people, but hardly of the expert in any particular field of knowledge. It is rather the person whose general knowledge is supposed to qualify him to appreciate expert testimony, and to judge between the experts from different fields, whose power is enhanced. The point which is important for us, however, is that the scholar who becomes a university president, the scientist who takes charge of an institute or foundation, the scholar who becomes an editor or the active promoter of an organization serving a particular cause, all rapidly cease to be scholars or experts and become intellectuals, solely in the light of certain fashionable general ideas. The number of such institutions which breed intellectuals and increase their number and powers grows every day. Almost all the "experts" in the mere technique of getting knowledge over are, with respect to the subject matter which they handle, intellectuals and not experts.

In the sense in which we are using the term, the intellectuals are in fact a fairly new phenomenon of history. Though nobody will regret that education has ceased to be a privilege of the propertied classes, the fact that the propertied classes are no longer the best educated, and the fact that the large number of people who owe their position solely to their general education do not possess that experience of the working of the economic system which the administration of property gives, are important to understanding the role of the intellectual. Professor Schumpeter, who has devoted an illuminating chapter of his *Capitalism, Socialism and Democracy* to some aspects of our problem, has not unfairly stressed that it is the absence of direct responsibility for practical affairs and the consequent absence of firsthand knowledge of them which distinguishes the typical intellectual from other people who also wield the power of the spoken and written word. It would lead too far, however, to examine here further the development of this class and the curious claim which has recently been advanced by one of its theorists that it was the only one whose views were not decidedly influenced by its own economic interests. One of the important points that would have to be examined in such a discussion would be how far the growth of this class has been artificially stimulated by the law of copyright.[1]

---

[1]It would be interesting to discover how far a seriously critical view of the benefits to society of the law of copyright or the expression of doubts about the public interest in the existence of a class which makes its living from the writing of books would have a chance of being publicly stated in a society in which the channels of expression are so largely controlled by people who have a vested interest in the existing situation.

III

It is not surprising that the real scholar or expert and the practical man of affairs often feel contemptuous about the intellectual, are disinclined to recognize his power, and are resentful when they discover it. Individually they find the intellectuals mostly to be people who understand nothing in particular especially well, and whose judgment on matters they themselves understand shows little sign of special wisdom. But it would be a fatal mistake to underestimate their power for this reason. Even though their knowledge may often be superficial and their intelligence limited, this does not alter the fact that it is their judgment which mainly determines the views on which society will act in the not too distant future. It is no exaggeration to say that once the more active part of the intellectuals have been converted to a set of beliefs, the process by which these become generally accepted is almost automatic and irresistible. They are the organs which modern society has developed for spreading knowledge and ideas and it is their convictions and opinions which operate as the sieve through which all new conceptions must pass before they can reach the masses.

It is of the nature of the intellectual's job that he must use his own knowledge and convictions in performing his daily task. He occupies his position because he possesses, or has had to deal from day to day with, knowledge which his employer in general does not possess, and his activities can therefore be directed by others only to a limited extent. And just because the intellectuals are mostly intellectually honest it is inevitable that they should follow their own convictions whenever they have discretion and that they should give a corresponding slant to everything that passes through their hands. Even where the direction of policy is in the hand of men of affairs of different views, the execution of policy will in general be in the hand of intellectuals, and it is frequently the decision on the detail which determines the net effect. We find this illustrated in almost all fields of contemporary society. Newspapers in "capitalist" ownership, universities presided over by "reactionary" governing bodies, broadcasting systems owned by conservative governments have all been known to influence public opinion in the direction of socialism, because this was the conviction of the personnel. This has often happened not only in spite of but perhaps even because of the attempts of those at the top to control opinion and to impose principles of orthodoxy.

The effect of this filtering of ideas through the convictions of a class which is constitutionally disposed to certain views is by no means confined to the masses. Outside his special field the expert is generally no less dependent on this class and scarcely less influenced by their selection. The result of this is that today in most parts of the Western world even the most determined opponents of socialism derive from socialist sources their knowledge on most subjects on which they have no firsthand information. With many of the more general preconceptions of socialist thought the connection of their more practical proposals is by no means at once obvious, and in consequence many men who believe themselves to be determined opponents of that system of thought become in fact effective spreaders of its ideas. Who does not know the practical man who in his own field denounces socialism as "pernicious rot" but when he steps outside his subject spouts socialism like any left journalist?

In no other field has the predominant influence of the socialist intellectuals been felt more strongly during the last hundred years than in the contacts between different national civilizations. It would go far beyond the limits of this article to trace the causes and significance of the highly important fact that in the modern world the intellectuals provide almost the only approach to an international community. It is this which mainly accounts for the extraordinary spectacle that for generations the supposedly "capitalist" West has been lending its moral and material support almost exclusively to those ideological movements in countries farther east which aimed at undermining Western civilization; and that at the same time the information which the Western public has obtained about events in Central and Eastern Europe has almost inevitably been colored by a socialist bias. Many of the "educational" activities of the American forces of occupation in Germany have furnished clear and recent examples of this tendency.

IV

A proper understanding of the reasons which tend to incline so many of the intellectuals toward socialism is thus most important. The first point here which those who do not share this bias ought to face frankly is that it is neither selfish interests nor evil intentions but mostly honest convictions and good intentions which determine the intellectuals' views. In fact it is necessary to recognize that on the whole the typical intellectual is today more likely to be a socialist the more he is guided by good will and intelligence and that on the plane of purely intellectual argument he will generally be able to make out a better case than the majority of his opponents within his class. If we still think him wrong we must recognize that it may be genuine error which leads the well-meaning and intelligent people who occupy those key positions in our society to spread views which to us appear a threat to our civilization.[2] Nothing could be more important than

[2]It was therefore not (as has been suggested by one reviewer of *The Road to Serfdom*, Professor J. Schumpeter) "politeness to a fault" but profound conviction of the importance of this which made me, in

to try and understand the sources of this error in order that we should be able to counter it. Yet those who are generally regarded as the representatives of the existing order and who believe that they comprehend the dangers of socialism are usually very far from such understanding. They tend to regard the socialist intellectuals as nothing more than a pernicious bunch of highbrow radicals without appreciating their influence, and, by their whole attitude to them, tend to drive them even further into opposition to the existing order.

If we are to understand this peculiar bias of a large section of the intellectuals we must be clear about two points. The first is that they generally judge all particular issues exclusively in the light of certain general ideas; the second, that the characteristic errors of any age are frequently derived from some genuine new truths it has discovered, and they are erroneous applications of new generalizations which have proved their value in other fields. The conclusion to which we shall be led by a full consideration of these facts will be that the effective refutation of such errors will frequently require further intellectual advance, and often advance on points which are very abstract and may seem very remote from the practical issues.

It is perhaps the most characteristic feature of the intellectual that he judges new ideas not by their specific merits but by the readiness with which they fit into his general conceptions, into the picture of the world which he regards as modern or advanced. It is through their influence on him and on his choice of opinions on particular issues that the power of ideas for good and evil grows in proportion with their generality, abstractness,

---

Professor Schumpeter's words, "hardly ever attribute to opponents anything beyond intellectual error."

and even vagueness. As he knows little about the particular issues, his criterion must be consistency with his other views, suitability to combine them into a coherent picture of the world. Yet this selection from the multitude of new ideas presenting themselves at every moment creates the characteristic climate of opinion, the dominant *Weltanschauung* of a period which will be favorable to the reception of some opinions and unfavorable to others, and which will make the intellectual readily accept one conclusion and reject another without a real understanding of the issues.

In some respects the intellectual is indeed closer to the philosopher than to any specialist, and the philosopher is in more than one sense a sort of prince among the intellectuals. Although his influence is farther removed from practical affairs and correspondingly slower and more difficult to trace than that of the ordinary intellectual, it is of the same kind and in the long run even more powerful than that of the latter. It is the same endeavor toward a synthesis, pursued more methodically, the same judgment of particular views in so far as they fit into a general system of thought rather than by their specific merits, the same striving after a consistent world view, which for both forms the main basis for accepting or rejecting ideas. For this reason the philosopher has probably a greater influence over the intellectuals than any other scholar or scientist, and more than anyone else determines the manner in which the intellectuals exercise their censorship function. The popular influence of the scientific specialist begins to rival that of the philosopher only when he ceases to be a specialist and commences to philosophize about the progress of his subject—and usually only after he has been taken up by the intellectuals for reasons which have little to do with his scientific eminence.

The "climate of opinion" of any period is thus essentially a set of very general preconceptions by which the intellectual judges the importance of new facts and opinions. These preconceptions are mainly applications to what seem to him the most significant aspects of scientific achievements, a transfer to other fields of what has particularly impressed him in the work of the specialists. One could give a long list of such intellectual fashions and catchwords which in the course of two or three generations have in turn dominated the thinking of the intellectuals. Whether it was the "historical approach" or the theory of evolution, nineteenth century determinism and the belief in the predominant influence of environment as against heredity, the theory of relativity or the belief in the power of the unconscious—every one of these general conceptions has been made the touchstone by which innovations in different fields have been tested. It seems as if the less specific or precise (or the less understood) these ideas are, the wider may be their influence. Sometimes it is no more than a vague impression rarely put into words which thus wields a profound influence. Such beliefs as that deliberate control or conscious organization is also in social affairs always superior to the results of spontaneous processes which are not directed by a human mind, or that any order based on a plan laid down beforehand must be better than one formed by the balancing of opposing forces, have in this way profoundly affected political development.

Only apparently different is the role of the intellectuals where the development of more properly social ideas is concerned. Here their peculiar propensities manifest themselves in making shibboleths of abstractions, in rationalizing and carrying to extremes certain ambitions which spring from the normal intercourse of men. Since democracy is a good thing, the further the democratic principle can be carried, the better it appears to them. The most powerful of these general ideas which have shaped political development in recent times is of course the ideal of material equality. It is, characteristically, not one of the spontaneously grown moral convictions, first applied in the relations between particular individuals, but an intellectual construction originally conceived in the abstract and of doubtful meaning or application in particular instances. Nevertheless, it has operated strongly as a principle of selection among the alternative courses of social policy, exercising a persistent pressure toward an arrangement of social affairs which nobody clearly conceives. That a particular measure tends to bring about greater equality has come to be regarded as so strong a recommendation that little else will be considered. Since on each particular issue it is this one aspect on which those who guide opinion have a definite conviction, equality has determined social change even more strongly than its advocates intended.

Not only moral ideals act in this manner, however. Sometimes the attitudes of the intellectuals toward the problems of social order may be the consequence of advances in purely scientific knowledge and it is in these instances that their erroneous views on particular issues may for a time seem to have all the prestige of the latest scientific achievements behind them. It is not in itself surprising that a genuine advance of knowledge should in this manner become on occasion a source of new error. If no false conclusions followed from new generalizations they would be final truths which would never need revision. Although as a rule such a new generalization will merely share the false consequences which can be drawn from it with the views which were held before, and thus not lead to *new* error, it is quite likely that a new theory, just as its value is shown by the valid new conclusions to which it leads, will produce other new conclusions which further advance will show to have been erroneous. But in such an instance a false belief will appear with all the prestige of the latest scientific knowledge supporting it. Although in the particular field to which this belief applies all the scientific evidence may be against it, it will nevertheless, before the tribunal of the intellectuals and in the light of the ideas which govern their thinking, be selected as the view which is best in accord with the spirit of the time. The specialists who will thus achieve public fame and wide influence will thus not be those who have gained recognition by their peers but will often be men whom the other experts regard as cranks, amateurs, or even frauds, but who in the eyes of the general public nevertheless become the best known exponents of their subject.

In particular, there can be little doubt that the manner in which during the last hundred years man has learned to organize the forces of nature has contributed a great deal toward the creation of the belief that a similar control of the forces of society would bring comparable improvements in human conditions. That, with the application of engineering techniques, the direction of all forms of human activity according to a single coherent plan should prove to be as successful in society as it has been in innumerable engineering tasks is too plausible a conclusion not to seduce most of those who are elated by the achievement of the natural sciences. It must indeed be admitted both that it would require powerful arguments to counter the strong presumption in favor of such a conclusion and that these arguments have not yet been adequately stated. It is not sufficient to point out the defects of particular proposals based on this kind of reasoning. The argument will not lose its force until it has been conclusively shown why what has proved so eminently successful in producing advances in so many fields should have limits to its usefulness and become positively harmful if extended beyond these limits. This is a task which has not yet been satisfactorily performed and which will have to be achieved before this particular impulse toward socialism can be removed.

This, of course, is only one of many instances where further intellectual advance is needed if the harmful ideas at present current are to be refuted, and where the course which we shall travel will ultimately be decided by the discussion of very abstract issues. It is not enough for the man of affairs to be sure, from his intimate knowledge of a particular field, that the theories of socialism which are derived from more general ideas will prove impracticable. He may be perfectly right, and yet his resistance will be overwhelmed and all the sorry consequences which he foresees will follow if he is not supported by an effective refutation of the *idées mères*. So long as the intellectual gets the better of the general argument, the most valid objections of the specific issue will be brushed aside.

V

This is not the whole story, however. The forces which influence recruitment to the ranks of the intellectuals operate in the same direction and help to explain why so many of the most able among them lean toward socialism. There are of course as many differences of opinion among intellectuals as among other groups of people; but it seems to be true that it is on the whole the more active, intelligent, and original men among the intellectuals who most frequently incline toward socialism, while its opponents are often of an inferior caliber. This is true particularly during the early stages of the infiltration of socialist ideas; later, although outside intellectual circles it may still be an act of courage to profess socialist convictions, the pressure of opinion among intellectuals will often be so strongly in favor of socialism that it requires more strength and independence for a man to resist it than to join in what his fellows regard as modern views. Nobody, for instance, who is familiar with large numbers of university faculties (and from this point of view the majority of university teachers probably have to be classed as intellectuals rather than as experts) can remain oblivious to the fact that the most brilliant and successful teachers are today more likely than not to be socialists, while those who hold more conservative political views are as frequently mediocrities. This is of course by itself an important factor leading the younger generation into the socialist camp.

The socialist will, of course, see in this merely a proof that the more intelligent person is today bound to become a socialist. But this is far from being the necessary or even the most likely explanation. The main reason for this state of affairs is probably that, for the exceptionally able man who accepts the present order of society, a multitude of other avenues to influence and power are open, while to the disaffected and dissatisfied an intellectual career is the most promising path to both influence and the power to contribute to the achievement of his ideals. Even more than that: the more conservatively inclined man of first class ability will in general choose intellectual work (and the sacrifice in material reward which this choice usually entails) only if he enjoys it for its own sake. He is in consequence more likely to become an expert scholar rather than an intellectual in the specific sense of the word; while to the more radically minded the intellectual pursuit is more often than not a means rather than an end, a path to exactly that kind of wide influence which the professional intellectual exercises. It is therefore probably the fact, not that the more intelligent people are generally socialists, but that a much higher proportion of socialists among the best minds devote themselves to those intellectual pursuits which in modern society give them a decisive influence on public opinion.[3]

---

[3]Related to this is another familiar phenomenon: there is little reason to believe that really first class intellectual ability for original work

The selection of the personnel of the intellectuals is also closely connected with the predominant interest which they show in general and abstract ideas. Speculations about the possible entire reconstruction of society give the intellectual a fare much more to his taste than the more practical and short-run considerations of those who aim at a piecemeal improvement of the existing order. In particular, socialist thought owes its appeal to the young largely to its visionary character; the very courage to indulge in Utopian thought is in this respect a source of strength to the socialists which traditional liberalism sadly lacks. This difference operates in favor of socialism, not only because speculation about general principles provides an opportunity for the play of the imagination of those who are unencumbered by much knowledge of the facts of present-day life, but also because it satisfies a legitimate desire for the understanding of the rational basis of any social order and gives scope for the exercise of that constructive urge for which liberalism, after it had won its great victories, left few outlets. The intellectual, by his whole disposition, is uninterested in technical details or practical difficulties. What appeal to him are the broad visions, the specious comprehension of the social order as a whole which a planned system promises.

This fact that the tastes of the intellectual were better satisfied by the speculations of the socialists proved fatal to the influence of the liberal tradition. Once the basic

---

is any rarer among Gentiles than among Jews. Yet there can be little doubt that men of Jewish stock almost everywhere constitute a disproportionately large number of the intellectuals in our sense, that is of the ranks of the professional interpreters of ideas. This may be their special gift and certainly is their main opportunity in countries where prejudice puts obstacles in their way in other fields. It is probably more because they constitute so large a proportion of the intellectuals than for any other reason that they seem to be so much more receptive of socialist ideas than people of different stocks.

demands of the liberal programs seemed satisfied, the liberal thinkers turned to problems of detail and tended to neglect the development of the general philosophy of liberalism, which in consequence ceased to be a live issue offering scope for general speculation. Thus for something over half a century it has been only the socialists who have offered anything like an explicit program of social development, a picture of the future society at which they were aiming, and a set of general principles to guide decisions on particular issues. Even though, if I am right, their ideals suffer from inherent contradictions, and any attempt to put them into practice must produce something utterly different from what they expect, this does not alter the fact that their program for change is the only one which has actually influenced the development of social institutions. It is because theirs has become the only explicit general philosophy of social policy held by a large group, the only system or theory which raises new problems and opens new horizons, that they have succeeded in inspiring the imagination of the intellectuals.

The actual developments of society during this period were determined, not by a battle of conflicting ideals, but by the contrast between an existing state of affairs and that one ideal of a possible future society which the socialists alone held up before the public. Very few of the other programs which offered themselves provided genuine alternatives. Most of them were mere compromises or half-way houses between the more extreme types of socialism and the existing order. All that was needed to make almost any socialist proposal appear reasonable to these "judicious" minds which were constitutionally convinced that the truth must always lie in the middle between the extremes was for someone to advocate a sufficiently more extreme proposal. There seemed to exist only one direction in which we could move and the only question seemed to be how fast and how far the movement should proceed.

VI

The significance of the special appeal to the intellectuals which socialism derives from its speculative character will become clearer if we further contrast the position of the socialist theorist with that of his counterpart who is a liberal in the old sense of the word. This comparison will also lead us to whatever lesson we can draw from an adequate appreciation of the intellectual forces which are undermining the foundations of a free society.

Paradoxically enough, one of the main handicaps which deprives the liberal thinker of popular influence is closely connected with the fact that until socialism has actually arrived he has more opportunity of directly influencing decisions on current policy and that in consequence he is not only not tempted into that long run speculation which is the strength of the socialists, but actually discouraged from it, because any effort of this kind is likely to reduce the immediate good he can do. Whatever power he has to influence practical decisions he owes to his standing with the representatives of the existing order, and this standing he would endanger if he devoted himself to the kind of speculation which would appeal to the intellectuals and which through them could influence developments over longer periods. In order to carry weight with the powers that be he has to be "practical," "sensible," and "realistic." So long as he concerns himself with the immediate issues he is rewarded with influence, material success, and popularity with those who up to a point share his general outlook. But these men have little respect for those speculations on general principles which shape the intellectual climate. Indeed, if he seriously indulges in such long run speculation he is apt to acquire the reputation of being "unsound" or even half a socialist, because he is unwilling to identify the existing order with the free system at which he aims.[4]

If, in spite of this, his efforts continue in the direction of general speculation, he soon discovers that it is unsafe to associate too closely with those who seem to share most of his convictions and he is soon driven into isolation. Indeed there can be few more thankless tasks at present than the essential one of developing the philosophical foundation on which the further development of a free society must be based. Since the man who undertakes it must accept much of the framework of the existing order, he will appear to many of the more speculatively minded intellectuals merely as a timid apologist of things as they are; at the same time he will be dismissed by the men of affairs as an impractical theorist. He is not radical enough for those who know only the world where "with ease together dwell the thoughts" and much too radical for those who see only how "hard in space together clash the things." If he takes advantage of such support as he can get from the men of affairs, he will almost certainly discredit himself with those on whom he depends for the spreading of his ideas. At the same time he will need most carefully to avoid anything resembling extravagance or overstatement. While no socialist theorist has ever been known to

[4]The most glaring recent example of such condemnation of a somewhat unorthodox liberal work as "socialist" has been provided by some comments on the late Henry Simons' *Economic Policy for a Free Society* (1948). One need not agree with the whole of this work and one may even regard some of the suggestions made in it as incompatible with a free society, and yet recognize it as one of the most important contributions made in recent times to our problem and as just the kind of work which is required to get discussion started on the fundamental issues. Even those who violently disagree with some of its suggestions should welcome it as a contribution which clearly and courageously raises the central problems of our time.

discredit himself with his fellows even by the silliest of proposals, the old-fashioned liberal will damn himself by an impracticable suggestion. Yet for the intellectuals he will still not be speculative or adventurous enough and the changes and improvements in the social structure he will have to offer will seem limited in comparison with what their less restrained imagination conceives.

At least in a society in which the main requisites of freedom have already been won and further improvements must concern points of comparative detail, the liberal program can have none of the glamour of a new invention. The appreciation of the improvements it has to offer requires more knowledge of the working of the existing society than the average intellectual possesses. The discussion of these improvements must proceed on a more practical level than that of the more revolutionary programs, thus giving a complexion which has little appeal for the intellectual and tending to bring in elements to whom he feels directly antagonistic. Those who are most familiar with the working of the present society are also usually interested in the preservation of particular features of that society which may not be defensible on general principles. Unlike the person who looks for an entirely new future order and who naturally turns for guidance to the theorist, the men who believe in the existing order also usually think that they understand it much better than any theorist and in consequence are likely to reject whatever is unfamiliar and theoretical.

The difficulty of finding genuine and disinterested support for a systematic policy for freedom is not new. In a passage of which the reception of a recent book of mine has often reminded me, Lord Acton long ago described how "[a]t all times sincere friends of freedom have been rare, and its triumphs have been due to minorities, that have prevailed by associating themselves with auxiliaries whose objects differed from their own; and this association, which is always dangerous, has been sometimes disastrous, by giving to opponents just grounds of opposition. . . ."[5] More recently, one of the most distinguished living American economists has complained in a similar vein that the main task of those who believe in the basic principles of the capitalist system must frequently be to defend this system against the capitalists—indeed the great liberal economists, from Adam Smith to the present, have always known this.

The most serious obstacle which separates the practical men who have the cause of freedom genuinely at heart from those forces which in the realm of ideas decide the course of development is their deep distrust of theoretical speculation and their tendency to orthodoxy; this more than anything else creates an almost impassable barrier between them and those intellectuals who are devoted to the same cause and whose assistance is indispensable if the cause is to prevail. Although this tendency is perhaps natural among men who defend a system because it has justified itself in practice, and to whom its intellectual justification seems immaterial, it is fatal to its survival because it deprives it of the support it most needs. Orthodoxy of any kind, any pretense that a system of ideas is final and must be unquestioningly accepted as a whole, is the one view which of necessity antagonizes all intellectuals, whatever their views on particular issues. Any system which judges men by the completeness of their conformity to a fixed set of opinions, by their "soundness" or the extent to which they can be relied upon to hold approved views on all points, deprives itself of a support without which no set of ideas can maintain its influence in modern society. The ability to criticize accepted views, to explore new vistas and to experience with new conceptions, provides the atmosphere without which the intellectual cannot breathe.

---

[5] Acton, *The History of Freedom* I (1922).

A cause which offers no scope for these traits can have no support from him and is thereby doomed in any society which like ours rests on his services.

VII

It may be that as a free society as we have known it carries in itself the forces of its own destruction, that once freedom has been achieved it is taken for granted and ceases to be valued, and that the free growth of ideas which is the essence of a free society will bring about the destruction of the foundations on which it depends. There can be little doubt that in countries like the United States the ideal of freedom today has less real appeal for the young than it has in countries where they have learned what its loss means. On the other hand, there is every sign that in Germany and elsewhere, to the young men who have never known a free society, the task of constructing one can become as exciting and fascinating as any socialist scheme which has appeared during the last hundred years. It is an extraordinary fact, though one which many visitors have experienced, that in speaking to German students about the principles of a liberal society one finds a more responsive and even enthusiastic audience than one can hope to find in any of the Western democracies. In Britain also there is already appearing among the young a new interest in the principles of true liberalism which certainly did not exist a few years ago.

Does this mean that freedom is valued only when it is lost, that the world must everywhere go through a dark phase of socialist totalitarianism before the forces of freedom can gather strength anew? It may be so, but I hope it need not be. Yet so long as the people who over longer periods determine public opinion continue to be attracted by the ideals of socialism, the trend will continue. If we are to avoid such a development we must be able to offer a new liberal program which appeals to the imagination. We must make the building of a free society once more an intellectual adventure, a deed of courage. What we lack is a liberal Utopia, a program which seems neither a mere defense of things as they are nor a diluted kind of socialism, but truly liberal radicalism which does not spare the susceptibilities of the mighty (including the trade unions), which is not too severely practical, and which does not confine itself to what appears today as politically possible. We need intellectual leaders who are prepared to resist the blandishments of power and influence and who are willing to work for an ideal, however small may be the prospects of its early realization. They must be men who are willing to stick to principles and to fight for their full realization, however remote. The practical compromises they must leave to the politicians. Free trade and the freedom of opportunity are ideals which still may arouse the imaginations of large numbers, but a mere "reasonable freedom of trade" or a mere "relaxation of controls" is neither intellectually respectable nor likely to inspire any enthusiasm.

The main lesson which the true liberal must learn from the success of the socialists is that it was their courage to be Utopian which gained them the support of the intellectuals and therefore an influence on public opinion which is daily making possible what only recently seemed utterly remote. Those who have concerned themselves exclusively with what seemed practicable in the existing state of opinion have constantly found that even this has rapidly become politically impossible as the result of changes in a public opinion which they have done nothing to guide. Unless we can make the philosophic foundations of a free society once more a living intellectual issue, and its implementation a task which challenges the ingenuity and imagination of our liveliest minds, the prospects of freedom are indeed dark. But if we can regain that belief in the power of ideas which was the mark of liberalism at its greatest, the battle is not lost. The intellectual revival of liberalism is already under way in many parts of the world. Will it be in time?

CHAPTER 2

Why the Worst Get on Top*

All power corrupts, absolute power corrupts absolutely.

—Lord Acton[1]

We must now examine a belief from which many who regard the advent of totalitarianism as inevitable derive consolation and which seriously weakens the resistance of many others who would oppose it with all their might if they fully apprehended its nature. It is the belief that the most repellent features of the totalitarian regimes are due to the historical accident that they were established by groups of blackguards and thugs. Surely, it is argued, if in Germany the creation of a totalitarian regime brought the Streichers and Killingers, the Leys and Heines, the Himmlers and Heydrichs to power, this may prove the viciousness of the German character, but not that the rise of such people is the necessary consequence of a totalitarian system. Why

*This text is based on the version of this essay published as chapter 10 of *The Road to Serfdom, Text and Documents, The Definitive Edition*, vol. 2 of *The Collected Works of F. A. Hayek*, ed. Bruce Caldwell (Chicago: University of Chicago, 2007), pp. 157–70. Original text 1944 by the University of Chicago.

[1]Lord Acton, *Historical Essays and Studies*, ed. John Nevill Figgis and Reginald Vere Laurence (London: Macmillan, 1919), p. 504.

should it not be possible that the same sort of system, if it be necessary to achieve important ends, be run by decent people for the good of the community as a whole?

We must not deceive ourselves into believing that all good people must be democrats or will necessarily wish to have a share in the government. Many, no doubt, would rather entrust it to somebody whom they think more competent. Although this might be unwise, there is nothing bad or dishonorable in approving a dictatorship of the good. Totalitarianism, we can already hear it argued, is a powerful system alike for good and evil, and the purpose for which it will be used depends entirely on the dictators. And those who think that it is not the system which we need fear, but the danger that it might be run by bad men, might even be tempted to forestall this danger by seeing that it is established in time by good men.

No doubt an English "Fascist" system would greatly differ from the Italian or German models; no doubt if the transition were effected without violence, we might expect to get a better type of leader. And if I had to live under a Fascist system I have no doubt that I would rather live under one run by Englishmen than under one run by anybody else. Yet all this does not mean that, judged on our present standards, a British Fascist system would in the end prove so very different or much less intolerable than its prototypes. There are strong reasons for believing that what to us appear the worst features of the existing totalitarian systems are not accidental by-products, but phenomena which totalitarianism is certain sooner or later to produce. Just as the democratic statesman who sets out to plan economic life will soon be confronted with the alternative of either assuming dictatorial powers or abandoning his plans, so the totalitarian dictator would soon have to choose between disregard of ordinary morals and failure. It is for this reason that the unscrupulous and uninhibited are likely to be more successful in a society tending towards totalitarianism. Who does not see this has not yet grasped the full width of the gulf which separates totalitarianism from a liberal regime, the utter difference between the whole moral atmosphere under collectivism and the essentially individualist Western civilization.

The "moral basis of collectivism" has, of course, been much debated in the past; but what concerns us here is not its moral basis but its moral results. The usual discussions of the ethical aspects of collectivism refer to the question whether collectivism is demanded by existing moral convictions; or what moral convictions would be required if collectivism is to produce the hoped-for results. Our question, however, is what moral views will be produced by a collectivist organization of society, or what views are likely to rule it. The interaction between morals and institutions may well have the effect that the ethics produced by collectivism will be altogether different from the moral ideals that lead to the demand for collectivism. While we are apt to think that, since the desire for a collectivist system springs from high moral motives, such a system must be the breeding ground for the highest virtues, there is, in fact, no reason why any system should necessarily enhance those attitudes which serve the purpose for which it was designed. The ruling moral views will depend partly on the qualities that will lead individuals to success in a collectivist or totalitarian system, and partly on the requirements of the totalitarian machinery.

We must here return for a moment to the position which precedes the suppression of democratic institutions and the creation of a totalitarian regime. In this stage it is the general demand for quick and determined government action that is the dominating element in the situation, dissatisfaction with the slow and cumbersome course of democratic procedure which makes action for action's sake the goal. It is then the man or the party who seems strong and resolute enough "to get things done" who exercises the greatest appeal. "Strong" in this sense means not merely a numerical majority—it is the ineffectiveness of parliamentary majorities with which people are dissatisfied. What they will seek is somebody with such solid support as to inspire confidence that he can carry out whatever he wants. It is here that the new type of party, organized on military lines, comes in.

In the Central European countries the socialist parties had familiarized the masses with political organizations of a semi-military character designed to absorb as much as possible of the private life of the members. All that was wanted to give one group overwhelming power was to carry the same principle somewhat further, to seek strength not in the assured votes of huge numbers at occasional elections, but in the absolute and unreserved support of a smaller but more thoroughly organized body. The chance of imposing a totalitarian regime on a whole people depends on the leader first collecting round him a group which is prepared voluntarily to submit to that totalitarian discipline which they are to impose by force upon the rest.

Although the socialist parties had the strength to get anything if they had cared to use force, they were reluctant to do so. They had, without knowing it, set themselves a task which only the ruthless, ready to disregard the barriers of accepted morals, can execute.

That socialism can be put into practice only by methods which most socialists disapprove is, of course, a lesson learned by many social reformers in the past. The old socialist parties were inhibited by their democratic ideals; they did not possess the ruthlessness required for the performance of their chosen task. It is characteristic that both in Germany and Italy the success of Fascism was preceded by the refusal of the socialist parties to take over the responsibilities of government. They were unwilling wholeheartedly to employ the methods to which they had pointed the way. They still hoped for the miracle of a majority agreeing on a particular plan for the organization of the whole of society; others had already learned the lesson that in a planned society the question can no longer be on what a majority of the people agree, but what is the largest single group whose members agree sufficiently to make unified direction of all affairs possible; or, if no such group large enough to enforce its views exists, how it can be created and who will succeed in creating it.

There are three main reasons why such a numerous and strong group with fairly homogeneous views is not likely to be formed by the best but rather by the worst elements of any society. By our standards the principles on which such a group would be selected will be almost entirely negative.

In the first instance, it is probably true that in general the higher the education and intelligence of individuals becomes, the more their views and tastes are differentiated and the less likely they are to agree on a particular hierarchy of values. It is a corollary of this that if we wish to find a high degree of uniformity and similarity of outlook, we have to descend to the regions of lower moral and intellectual standards where the more primitive and "common" instincts and tastes prevail. This does not mean that the majority of people have low moral standards; it merely means that the largest group of people whose values are very similar are the people with low standards. It is, as it were, the lowest common denominator which unites the largest number of people. If a numerous group is needed, strong enough to impose their views on the values of life on all the rest, it will never be those with highly differentiated and developed tastes—it will be those who form the "mass" in the derogatory sense of the term, the least original and independent, who will be able to put the weight of their numbers behind their particular ideals.

If, however, a potential dictator had to rely entirely on those whose uncomplicated and primitive instincts happen to be very similar, their number would scarcely give sufficient weight to their endeavors. He will have to increase their numbers by converting more to the same simple creed.

Here comes in the second negative principle of selection: he will be able to obtain the support of all the docile and gullible, who have no strong convictions of their own but are prepared to accept a ready-made system of values if it is only drummed into their ears sufficiently loudly and frequently. It will be those whose vague and imperfectly formed ideas are easily swayed and whose passions and emotions are readily aroused who will thus swell the ranks of the totalitarian party.

It is in connection with the deliberate effort of the skillful demagogue to weld together a closely coherent and homogeneous body of supporters that the third and perhaps most important negative element of selection enters. It seems to be almost a law of human nature that it is easier for people to agree on a negative program, on the hatred of an enemy, on the envy of those better off, than on any positive task. The contrast between the "we" and the "they," the common fight against those outside the group, seems to be an essential ingredient in any creed which will solidly knit together a group for common action. It is consequently always employed by those who seek, not merely support of a policy, but the unreserved allegiance of huge masses. From their point of view it has the great advantage of leaving them greater freedom of action than almost any positive program. The enemy, whether he be internal like the "Jew" or the "Kulak," or external, seems to be an indispensable requisite in the armory of a totalitarian leader.

That in Germany it was the Jew who became the enemy till his place was taken by the "plutocracies" was no less a result of the anti-capitalist resentment on which the whole movement was based than the selection of the Kulak in Russia. In Germany and Austria the Jew had come to be regarded as the representative of capitalism because a traditional dislike of large classes of the population for commercial pursuits had left these more readily accessible to a group that was practically excluded from the more highly esteemed occupations. It is the old story of the alien race being admitted only to the less respected trades and then being hated still more for practicing them. The fact that German anti-semitism and anti-capitalism spring from the same root is of great importance for the understanding of what has happened there, but this is rarely grasped by foreign observers.

To treat the universal tendency of collectivist policy to become nationalistic as due entirely to the necessity for securing unhesitating support would be to neglect another and no less important factor. It may indeed be questioned whether anybody can realistically conceive of a collectivist program other than in the service of a limited group, whether collectivism can exist in any other form than that of some kind of particularism, be it nationalism, racialism, or class-ism. The belief in the community of aims and interests with fellow-men seems to presuppose a greater degree of similarity of outlook and thought than exists between men merely as human beings. If the other members of one's group cannot all be personally known, they must at least be of the same kind as those around us, think and talk in the same way and about the same kind of things, in order that we may identify ourselves with them. Collectivism on a world scale seems to be unthinkable—except in the service of a small ruling elite. It would certainly raise not only technical but above all moral problems which none of our socialists are willing to face. If the English proletarian is entitled to an equal share of the income now derived from England's capital resources, and of the control of their use, because they are the result of exploitation, so on the same principle all the Indians would be entitled not only to the income from but also to the use of a proportional share of the British capital. But what socialists seriously contemplate the equal division of existing capital resources among the people of the world? They all regard the capital as belonging not to humanity but to the nation—though even within the nation few would dare to advocate that the richer regions should be deprived of some of "their" capital equipment in order to help the poorer regions. What socialists proclaim as a duty towards the fellow members of the existing states, they are not prepared to grant to the foreigner. From a consistent collectivist point of view the claims of the "Have-Not" nations for a new division of the world are entirely justified—though, if consistently applied, those who demand it most loudly would lose by it almost as much as the richest nations. They are, therefore, careful not to base their claims on any equalitarian principles but on their pretended superior capacity to organize other peoples.

One of the inherent contradictions of the collectivist philosophy is, that while basing itself on the humanistic morals which individualism has developed, it is practicable only within a relatively small group. That socialism so long as it remains theoretical is internationalist, while as soon as it is put into practice, whether in Russia or in Germany, it becomes violently nationalist is one of the reasons why "liberal socialism" as most people in the Western world imagine it is purely theoretical, while the practice of socialism is everywhere totalitarian.[2] Collectivism has no room for the wide humanitarianism of liberalism but only for the narrow particularism of the totalitarian.

If the "community" and the state are prior to the individual, if they have ends of their own independent of and superior to those of the individuals, only those individuals who work for the same ends can be regarded as members of the community. It is a necessary consequence of this view that a person is respected only as a member of the group, that is, only if and in so far as he works for the recognized common ends, and that he derives his whole dignity only from this membership and not merely from being man. Indeed, the very concepts of humanity and therefore of any form of internationalism are entirely products of the individualist view of man, and there can be no place for them in a collectivist system of thought.[3]

Apart from the basic fact that the community of collectivism can extend only as far as the unity of purpose of the individuals exists or can be created, several contributory factors strengthen the tendency of collectivism to become particularist and exclusive. Of these one of the most important is that the desire of the individual to identify himself with a group is very frequently the result of a feeling of inferiority, and that therefore his want

---

[2]Cf. now the instructive discussion in F. Borkenau, *Socialism, National or International?*, 1942.

[3]It is entirely in the spirit of collectivism when Nietzsche makes his Zarathustra say:

> "A thousand goals have existed hitherto, for a thousand people existed. But the fetter for the thousand necks is still lacking, the one goal is still lacking. Humanity has no goal yet.
>
> "But tell me, I pray, my brethren: if the goal be lacking to humanity, is not humanity itself lacking?"

will only be satisfied if membership in the group confers some superiority over outsiders. Sometimes, it seems, the very fact that these violent instincts which the individual knows he must curb within the group can be given a free range in the collective action towards the outsider becomes a further inducement for merging personality in that of the group. There is a profound truth expressed in the title of R. Niebuhr's *Moral Man and Immoral Society*—however little we can follow him in the conclusions he draws from his thesis. There is indeed, as he says elsewhere, "an increasing tendency among modern men to imagine themselves ethical because they have delegated their vices to larger and larger groups."[4] To act on behalf of a group seems to free people of many of the moral restraints which control their behavior as individuals within the group.

The definitely antagonistic attitude which most planners take towards internationalism is further explained by the fact that in the existing world all outside contacts of a group are obstacles to their effectively planning the sphere in which they can attempt it. It is therefore no accident that, as the editor of one of the most comprehensive collective studies on planning has discovered to his chagrin, "most 'planners' are militant nationalists."[5]

The nationalist and imperialist propensities of socialist planners, much more common than is generally recognized, are not always as flagrant as, for example, in the case of the Webbs and some of the other early Fabians, with whom enthusiasm for planning was characteristically combined with the veneration for the large and powerful

---

4Quoted from an article of Dr. Niebuhr's by E. H. Carr, *The Twenty Years' Crisis*, 1941, p. 203.

5Findlay MacKenzie (ed.), *Planned Society, Yesterday, Today, Tomorrow: A Symposium*, 1937, p. xx.

political units and a contempt for the small state. The historian Elie Halévy, speaking of the Webbs when he first knew them forty years ago, records that

> their socialism was profoundly anti-liberal. They did not hate the Tories, indeed they were extraordinarily lenient to them, but they had no mercy for Gladstonian Liberalism. It was the time of the Boer War and both the advanced liberals and the men who were beginning to form the Labour Party had generously sided with the Boers against British Imperialism, in the name of freedom and humanity. But the two Webbs and their friend, Bernard Shaw, stood apart. They were ostentatiously imperialistic. The independence of small nations might mean something to the liberal individualist. It meant nothing to collectivists like themselves. I can still hear Sidney Webb explaining to me that the future belonged to the great administrative nations, where the officials govern and the police keep order.

And elsewhere Halévy quotes Bernard Shaw arguing, about the same time, that "the world is to the big and powerful states by necessity; and the little ones must come within their border or be crushed out of existence."[6]

I have quoted at length these passages, which would not surprise one in a description of the German ancestors of National Socialism, because they provide so characteristic an example of that glorification of power which easily leads from socialism to nationalism and which profoundly affects the ethical views of all collectivists. So far

---

[6]E. Halévy, *L'Ere des Tyrannies*, Paris, 1938, p. 217, and *History of the English People*, Epilogue, vol. I, pp. 105–6.

as the rights of small nations are concerned, Marx and Engels were little better than most other consistent collectivists, and the views they occasionally expressed about Czechs or Poles resemble those of contemporary National Socialists.[7]

While to the great individualist social philosophers of the nineteenth century, to a Lord Acton or Jacob Burckhardt, down to contemporary socialists, like Bertrand Russell, who have inherited the liberal tradition, power itself has always appeared the arch-evil, to the strict collectivist it is a goal in itself. It is not only, as Russell has so well described, that the desire to organize social life according to a unitary plan itself springs largely from a desire for power.[8] It is even more the outcome of the fact that in order to achieve their end collectivists must create power—power over men wielded by other men—of a magnitude never before known, and that their success will depend on the extent to which they achieve such power.

This remains true even though many liberal socialists are guided in their endeavors by the tragic illusion that by depriving private individuals of the power they possess in an individualist system, and by transferring this power to society, they can thereby extinguish power. What all those who argue in this manner overlook is that by concentrating power so that it can be used in the service of a single plan, it is not merely transferred but infinitely heightened; that by uniting in the hands of some single body power formerly exercised independently by many, an amount of power is created infinitely greater than any that existed before, so much more far-reaching as almost to be different in kind.

---

[7]Cf. K. Marx, *Revolution and Counter-revolution*, and Engels' letter to Marx, May 23, 1851.

[8]Bertrand Russell, *The Scientific Outlook*, 1931, p. 211.

It is entirely fallacious when it is sometimes argued that the great power exercised by a Central Planning Board would be "no greater than the power collectively exercised by private boards of directors."[9] There is, in a competitive society, nobody who can exercise even a fraction of the power which a socialist planning board would possess, and if nobody can consciously use the power, it is just an abuse of words to assert that it rests with all the capitalists put together.[10] It is merely a play upon words to speak of the "power collectively exercised by private boards of directors" so long as they do not combine to concerted action—which would, of course, mean the end of competition and the creation of a planned economy. To split or decentralize power is necessarily to reduce the absolute amount of power and the competitive system is the only system designed to minimize by decentralization the power exercised by man over man.

We have seen before how the separation of economic and political aims is an essential guarantee of individual freedom and how it is consequently attacked by all collectivists. To this we must now add that the "substitution of political for economic power" now so often demanded means necessarily the substitution of power from which there is no escape for a power which is always limited. What is called economic power, while it can be an instrument of coercion, is in the hands of private individuals never exclusive or complete power, never power over the

---

[9]B. E. Lippincott, in his Introduction to O. Lange and F. M. Taylor, *On the Economic Theory of Socialism*, Minneapolis, 1938, p. 33.

[10]We must not allow ourselves to be deceived by the fact that the word power, apart from the sense in which it is used with respect to human beings, is also used in an impersonal (or rather anthropomorphic) sense for any determining cause. Of course there will always be something that determines everything that happens, and in this sense the amount of power existing must always be the same. But this is not true of the power consciously wielded by human beings.

whole life of a person. But centralized as an instrument of political power it creates a degree of dependence scarcely distinguishable from slavery.

From the two central features of every collectivist system, the need for a commonly accepted system of ends of the group, and the all-overriding desire to give to the group the maximum of power to achieve these ends, grows a definite system of morals, which on some points coincides and on others violently contrasts with ours—but differs from it in one point which makes it doubtful whether we can call it morals: that it does not leave the individual conscience free to apply its own rules and does not even know any general rules which the individual is required or allowed to observe in all circumstances. This makes collectivist morals so different from what we have known as morals that we find it difficult to discover any principle in them, which they nevertheless possess.

The difference of principle is very much the same as that which we have already considered in connection with the Rule of Law. Like formal law the rules of individualist ethics, however unprecise they may be in many respects, are general and absolute; they prescribe or prohibit a general type of action irrespective of whether in the particular instance the ultimate purpose is good or bad. To cheat or steal, to torture or betray a confidence, is held to be bad, irrespective of whether or not in the particular instance any harm follows from it. Neither the fact that in a given instance nobody may be the worse for it, nor any high purpose for which such an act may have been committed, can alter the fact that it is bad. Though we may sometimes be forced to choose between different evils they remain evils. The principle that the end justifies the means is in individualist ethics regarded as the denial of all morals. In collectivist ethics it becomes necessarily the supreme rule; there is literally nothing which the consistent collectivist must not be prepared to do if it serves "the good of the whole," because the "good of the whole" is to him the only criterion of what ought to be done. The *raison d'état*, in which collectivist ethics has found its most explicit formulation, knows no other limit than that set by expediency—the suitability of the particular act for the end in view. And what the *raison d'état* affirms with respect to the relations between different countries applies equally to the relations between different individuals within the collectivist state. There can be no limit to what its citizen must be prepared to do, no act which his conscience must prevent him from committing, if it is necessary for an end which the community has set itself or which his superiors order him to achieve.

The absence of absolute formal rules in collectivist ethics does not, of course, mean that there are not some useful habits of the individuals which a collectivist community will encourage, and others which it will discourage. Quite the reverse; it will take a much greater interest in the individual's habits of life than an individualist community. To be a useful member of a collectivist society requires very definite qualities which must be strengthened by constant practice. The reason why we designate these qualities as "useful habits" and can hardly describe them as moral virtues is that the individual could never be allowed to put these rules above any definite orders, or to let them become an obstacle to the achievement of any of the particular aims of his community. They only serve, as it were, to fill any gaps which direct orders or the designation of particular aims may leave, but they can never justify a conflict with the will of the authority.

The differences between the virtues which will continue to be esteemed under a collectivist system and those which will disappear is well illustrated by a comparison of the virtues which even their worst enemies admit the Germans, or rather the "typical Prussian," to possess, and those of which they are commonly thought lacking and in which the English people, with some justification, used to pride themselves as excelling. Few people will deny that the Germans on the whole are industrious and disciplined, thorough and energetic to the degree of ruthlessness, conscientious and single-minded in any tasks they undertake, that they possess a strong sense of order, duty, and strict obedience to authority, and that they often show great readiness to make personal sacrifices and great courage in physical danger. All these make the German an efficient instrument in carrying out an assigned task, and they have accordingly been carefully nurtured in the old Prussian state and the new Prussian-dominated Reich. What the "typical German" is often thought to lack are the individualist virtues of tolerance and respect for other individuals and their opinions, of independence of mind and that uprightness of character and readiness to defend one's own convictions against a superior which the Germans themselves, usually conscious that they lack it, call *Zivilcourage*, of consideration for the weak and infirm, and of that healthy contempt and dislike of power which only an old tradition of personal liberty creates. Deficient they seem also in most of those little yet so important qualities which facilitate the intercourse between men in a free society: kindliness and a sense of humor, personal modesty, and respect for the privacy and belief in the good intentions of one's neighbor.

After what we have already said it will not cause surprise that these individualist virtues are at the same time eminently social virtues, virtues which smooth social contacts and which make control from above less necessary and at the same time more difficult. They are virtues which flourish wherever the individualist or commercial type of society has prevailed and which are missing according as the collectivist or military type of society predominates—a difference which is, or was, as noticeable between the various regions of Germany as it has now become between the views which rule in Germany and those characteristic of the West. Till recently, at least, in those parts of Germany which have been longest exposed to the civilizing forces of commerce, the old commercial towns of the south and west and the Hanse towns, the general moral concepts were probably much more akin to those of the Western people than to those which have now become dominant all over Germany.

It would, however, be highly unjust to regard the masses of the totalitarian people as devoid of moral fervor because they give unstinted support to a system which to us seems a denial of most moral values. For the great majority of them the opposite is probably true: the intensity of the moral emotions behind a movement like that of National Socialism or communism can probably be compared only to those of the great religious movements of history. Once you admit that the individual is merely a means to serve the ends of the higher entity called society or the nation, most of those features of totalitarian regimes which horrify us follow of necessity. From the collectivist standpoint intolerance and brutal suppression of dissent, the complete disregard of the life and happiness of the individual, are essential and unavoidable consequences of this basic premise, and the collectivist can admit this and at the same time claim that his system is superior to one in which the "selfish" interests of the individual are allowed to obstruct the full realization of the ends the community pursues. When German philosophers again and again represent the striving for personal happiness as itself immoral and only the fulfillment of an imposed duty as praiseworthy, they are perfectly sincere, however difficult this may be to understand for those who have been brought up in a different tradition.

Where there is one common all-overriding end there is no room for any general morals or rules. To a limited extent we ourselves experience this in wartime. But even war and the greatest peril had led in this country only to a very moderate approach to totalitarianism, very little setting aside of all other values in the service of a single purpose. But where a few specific ends dominate the whole of society, it is inevitable that occasionally cruelty may become a duty, that acts which revolt all our feeling, such as the shooting of hostages or the killing of the old or sick, should be treated as mere matters of expediency, that the compulsory uprooting and transportation of hundreds of thousands should become an instrument of policy approved by almost everybody except the victims, or that suggestions like that of a "conscription of women for breeding purposes" can be seriously contemplated. There is always in the eyes of the collectivist a greater goal which these acts serve and which to him justifies them because the pursuit of the common end of society can know no limits in any rights or values of any individual.

But while for the mass of the citizens of the totalitarian state it is often unselfish devotion to an ideal, although one that is repellent to us, which makes them approve and even perform such deeds, this cannot be pleaded for those who guide its policy. To be a useful assistant in the running of a totalitarian state it is not enough that a man should be prepared to accept specious justification of vile deeds; he must himself be prepared actively to break every moral rule he has ever known if this seems necessary to achieve the end set for him. Since it is the supreme leader who alone determines the ends, his instruments must have no moral convictions of their own. They must, above all, be unreservedly committed to the person of the leader; but next to this the most important thing is that they should be completely unprincipled and literally capable of everything. They must have no ideals of their own which they want to realize, no ideas about right or wrong which might interfere with the intentions of the leader. There is thus in the positions of power little to attract those who hold moral beliefs of the kind which in the past have guided the European peoples, little which could compensate for the distastefulness of many of the particular tasks, and little opportunity to gratify any more idealistic desires, to recompense for the undeniable risk, the sacrifice of most of the pleasures of private life and of personal independence which the posts of great responsibility involve. The only tastes which are satisfied are the taste for power as such, the pleasure of being obeyed and of being part of a well-functioning and immensely powerful machine to which everything else must give way.

Yet while there is little that is likely to induce men who are good by our standards to aspire to leading positions in the totalitarian machine, and much to deter them, there will be special opportunities for the ruthless and unscrupulous. There will be jobs to be done about the badness of which taken by themselves nobody has any doubt, but which have to be done in the service of some higher end, and which have to be executed with the same expertness and efficiency as any others. And as there will be need for actions which are bad in themselves, and which all those still influenced by traditional morals will be reluctant to perform, the readiness to do bad things becomes a path to promotion and power. The positions in a totalitarian society in which it is necessary to practice cruelty and intimidation, deliberate deception and spying, are numerous. Neither the Gestapo nor the administration of a concentration camp, neither the Ministry of Propaganda nor the SA or SS (or their Italian or Russian counterparts) are suitable places for the exercise of humanitarian feelings. Yet it is through positions like these that the road to the highest positions in the totalitarian state leads. It is only too true when a distinguished American economist concludes from a similar brief enumeration of the duties of the authorities of a collectivist state that

> they would have to do these things whether they wanted to or not: and the probability of the people in power being individuals who would dislike the possession and exercise of power is on a level with the probability that an extremely tenderhearted person would get the job of whipping-master in a slave plantation.[11]

We cannot, however, exhaust this subject here. The problem of the selection of the leaders is closely bound up with the wide problem of selection according to the opinions held, or rather according to the readiness with which a person conforms to an ever-changing set of doctrines. And this leads us to one of the most characteristic moral features of totalitarianism, its relation to, and its effect on, all the virtues falling under the general heading of truthfulness. This is so big a subject that it requires a separate chapter.

---

[11]Professor F. H. Knight in *The Journal of Political Economy*, December 1938, p. 869.

Chapter 3

The Use of Knowledge in Society*

I

What is the problem we wish to solve when we try to construct a rational economic order?

On certain familiar assumptions the answer is simple enough. *If* we possess all the relevant information, *if* we can start out from a given system of preferences, and *if* we command complete knowledge of available means, the problem which remains is purely one of logic. That is, the answer to the question of what is the best use of the available means is implicit in our assumptions. The conditions which the solution of this optimum problem must satisfy have been fully worked out and can be stated best in mathematical form: put at their briefest, they are that the marginal rates of substitution between any two commodities or factors must be the same in all their different uses.

This, however, is emphatically *not* the economic problem which society faces. And the economic calculus which we have developed to solve this logical problem,

*This text is based on the version of this essay published in *The American Economic Review* 35, no. 4 (1945): 519–30.

though an important step toward the solution of the economic problem of society, does not yet provide an answer to it. The reason for this is that the "data" from which the economic calculus starts are never for the whole society "given" to a single mind which could work out the implications, and can never be so given.

The peculiar character of the problem of a rational economic order is determined precisely by the fact that the knowledge of the circumstances of which we must make use never exists in concentrated or integrated form, but solely as the dispersed bits of incomplete and frequently contradictory knowledge which all the separate individuals possess. The economic problem of society is thus not merely a problem of how to allocate "given" resources—if "given" is taken to mean given to a single mind which deliberately solves the problem set by these "data." It is rather a problem of how to secure the best use of resources known to any of the members of society, for ends whose relative importance only these individuals know. Or, to put it briefly, it is a problem of the utilization of knowledge which is not given to anyone in its totality.

This character of the fundamental problem has, I am afraid, been obscured rather than illuminated by many of the recent refinements of economic theory, particularly by many of the uses made of mathematics. Though the problem with which I want primarily to deal in this paper is the problem of a rational economic organization, I shall in its course be led again and again to point to its close connections with certain methodological questions. Many of the points I wish to make are indeed conclusions toward which diverse paths of reasoning have unexpectedly converged. But as I now see these problems, this is no accident. It seems to me that many of the current disputes with regard to both economic theory and economic policy have their common origin in a misconception about the nature of the economic problem of society. This misconception in turn is due to an erroneous transfer to social phenomena of the habits of thought we have developed in dealing with the phenomena of nature.

II

In ordinary language we describe by the word "planning" the complex of interrelated decisions about the allocation of our available resources. All economic activity is in this sense planning; and in any society in which many people collaborate, this planning, whoever does it, will in some measure have to be based on knowledge which, in the first instance, is not given to the planner but to somebody else, and which somehow will have to be conveyed to the planner. The various ways in which the knowledge on which people base their plans is communicated to them is the crucial problem for any theory explaining the economic process. And the problem of what is the best way of utilizing knowledge initially dispersed among all the people is at least one of the main problems of economic policy—or of designing an efficient economic system.

The answer to this question is closely connected with that other question which arises here, that of *who* is to do the planning. It is about this question that all the dispute about "economic planning" centers. This is not a dispute about whether planning is to be done or not. It is a dispute as to whether planning is to be done centrally, by one authority for the whole economic system, or is to be divided among many individuals. Planning in the specific sense in which the term is used in contemporary controversy necessarily means central planning—direction of the whole economic system according to one unified plan. Competition, on the other hand, means decentralized planning by many separate persons. The half-way house between the two, about which many people talk but which few like when they see it, is the delegation of planning to organized industries, or, in other words, monopoly.

Which of these systems is likely to be more efficient depends mainly on the question of under which of them we can expect that fuller use will be made of the existing knowledge. And this, in turn, depends on whether we are more likely to succeed in putting at the disposal of a single central authority all the knowledge which ought to be used but which is initially dispersed among many different individuals, or in conveying to the individuals such additional knowledge as they need in order to enable them to fit their plans in with those of others.

III

It will at once be evident that on this point the position will be different with respect to different kinds of knowledge; and the answer to our question will therefore largely turn on the relative importance of the different kinds of knowledge; those more likely to be at the disposal of particular individuals and those which we should with greater confidence expect to find in the possession of an authority made up of suitably chosen experts. If it is today so widely assumed that the latter will be in a better position, this is because one kind of knowledge, namely, scientific knowledge, occupies now so prominent a place in public imagination that we tend to forget that it is not the only kind that is relevant. It may be admitted that, so far as scientific knowledge is concerned, a body of suitably chosen experts may be in the best position to command all the best knowledge available—though this is of course merely shifting the difficulty to the problem of selecting the experts. What I wish to point out is that, even assuming that this problem can be readily solved, it is only a small part of the wider problem.

Today it is almost heresy to suggest that scientific knowledge is not the sum of all knowledge. But a little reflection will show that there is beyond question a body of very important but unorganized knowledge which cannot possibly be called scientific in the sense of knowledge of general rules: the knowledge of the particular circumstances of time and place. It is with respect to this that practically every individual has some advantage over all others because he possesses unique information of which beneficial use might be made, but of which use can be made only if the decisions depending on it are left to him or are made with his active cooperation. We need only to remember how much we have to learn in any occupation after we have completed our theoretical training, how big a part of our working life we spend learning particular jobs, and how valuable an asset in all walks of life is knowledge of people, of local conditions, and of special circumstances. To know of and put to use a machine not fully employed, or somebody's skill which could be better utilized, or to be aware of a surplus stock which can be drawn upon during an interruption of supplies, is socially quite as useful as the knowledge of better alternative techniques. And the shipper who earns his living from using otherwise empty or half-filled journeys of tramp-steamers, or the estate agent whose whole knowledge is almost exclusively one of temporary opportunities, or the *arbitrageur* who gains from local differences of commodity prices, are all performing eminently useful functions based on special knowledge of circumstances of the fleeting moment not known to others.

It is a curious fact that this sort of knowledge should today be generally regarded with a kind of contempt, and that anyone who by such knowledge gains an advantage over somebody better equipped with theoretical or technical knowledge is thought to have acted almost disreputably. To gain an advantage from better knowledge of facilities of communication or transport is sometimes regarded as almost dishonest, although it is quite as important that society make use of the best opportunities in this respect as in using the latest scientific discoveries. This prejudice has in a considerable measure affected the attitude toward commerce in general compared with that toward production. Even economists who regard themselves as definitely above the crude materialist fallacies of the past constantly commit the same mistake where activities directed toward the acquisition of such practical knowledge are concerned—apparently because in their scheme of things all such knowledge is supposed to be "given." The common idea now seems to be that all such knowledge should as a matter of course be readily at the command of everybody, and the reproach of irrationality leveled against the existing economic order is frequently based on the fact that it is not so available. This view disregards the fact that the method by which such knowledge can be made as widely available as possible is precisely the problem to which we have to find an answer.

IV

If it is fashionable today to minimize the importance of the knowledge of the particular circumstances of time and place, this is closely connected with the smaller importance which is now attached to change as such. Indeed, there are few points on which the assumptions made (usually only implicitly) by the "planners" differ from those of their opponents as much as with regard to the significance and frequency of changes which will make substantial alterations of production plans necessary. Of course, if detailed economic plans could be laid down for fairly long periods in advance and then closely adhered to, so that no further economic decisions of importance would be required, the task of drawing up a comprehensive plan governing all economic activity would appear much less formidable.

It is, perhaps, worth stressing that economic problems arise always and only in consequence of change. So long as things continue as before, or at least as they were expected to, there arise no new problems requiring a decision, no need to form a new plan. The belief that changes, or at least day-to-day adjustments, have become less important in modern times implies the contention that economic problems also have become less important. This belief in the decreasing importance of change is, for that reason, usually held by the same people who argue that the importance of economic considerations has been driven into the background by the growing importance of technological knowledge.

Is it true that, with the elaborate apparatus of modern production, economic decisions are required only at long intervals, as when a new factory is to be erected or a new process to be introduced? Is it true that, once a plant has been built, the rest is all more or less mechanical, determined by the character of the plant, and leaving little to be changed in adapting to the ever-changing circumstances of the moment?

The fairly widespread belief in the affirmative is not, so far as I can ascertain, borne out by the practical experience of the business man. In a competitive industry at any rate—and such an industry alone can serve as a test—the task of keeping cost from rising requires constant struggle, absorbing a great part of the energy of the manager. How easy it is for an inefficient manager to dissipate the differentials on which profitability rests, and that it is possible, with the same technical facilities, to produce with a great variety of costs, are among the commonplaces of business experience which do not seem to be equally familiar in the study of the economist. The very strength of the desire, constantly voiced by producers and engineers, to be able to proceed untrammeled by considerations of money costs is eloquent testimony to the extent to which these factors enter into their daily work.

One reason why economists are increasingly apt to forget about the constant small changes which make up the whole economic picture is probably their growing preoccupation with statistical aggregates, which show a very much greater stability than the movements of the detail. The comparative stability of the aggregates cannot, however, be accounted for—as the statisticians occasionally seem to be inclined to do—by the "law of large numbers" or the mutual compensation of random changes. The number of elements with which we have to deal is not large enough for such accidental forces to produce stability. The continuous flow of goods and services is maintained by constant deliberate adjustments, by new dispositions made every day in the light of circumstances not known the day before, by *B* stepping in at once when *A* fails to deliver. Even the large and highly mechanized plant keeps going largely because of an environment upon which it can draw for all sorts of unexpected needs; tiles for its roof, stationery for its forms, and all the thousand and one kinds of equipment in which it cannot be self-contained and which the plans for the operation of the plant require to be readily available in the market.

This is, perhaps, also the point where I should briefly mention the fact that the sort of knowledge with which I have been concerned is knowledge of the kind which by its nature cannot enter into statistics and therefore cannot be conveyed to any central authority in statistical form. The statistics which such a central authority would have to use would have to be arrived at precisely by abstracting from minor differences between the things, by lumping together, as resources of one kind, items which differ as regards location, quality, and other particulars, in a way which may be very significant for the specific decision. It follows from this that central planning based on statistical information by its nature cannot take direct account of these circumstances of time and place, and that the central planner will have to find some way or other in which the decisions depending on them can be left to the "man on the spot."

V

If we can agree that the economic problem of society is mainly one of rapid adaptation to changes in the particular circumstances of time and place, it would seem to follow that the ultimate decisions must be left to the people who are familiar with these circumstances, who know directly of the relevant changes and of the resources immediately available to meet them. We cannot expect that this problem will be solved by first communicating all this knowledge to a central board which, after integrating *all* knowledge, issues its orders. We must solve it by some form of decentralization. But this answers only part of our problem. We need decentralization because only thus can we ensure that the knowledge of the particular circumstances of time and place will be promptly used. But the "man on the spot" cannot decide solely on the basis of his limited but intimate knowledge of the facts of his immediate surroundings. There still remains the problem of communicating to him such further information as he needs to fit his decisions into the whole pattern of changes of the larger economic system.

How much knowledge does he need to do so successfully? Which of the events which happen beyond the horizon of his immediate knowledge are of relevance to his immediate decision, and how much of them need he know?

There is hardly anything that happens anywhere in the world that *might* not have an effect on the decision he ought to make. But he need not know of these events as such, nor of *all* their effects. It does not matter for him *why* at the particular moment more screws of one size than of another are wanted, *why* paper bags are more readily available than canvas bags, or *why* skilled labor, or particular machine tools, have for the moment become more difficult to acquire. All that is significant for him is *how much more or less* difficult to procure they have become compared with other things with which he is also concerned, or how much more or less urgently wanted are the alternative things he produces or uses. It is always a question of the relative importance of the particular things with which he is concerned, and the causes which alter their relative importance are of no interest to him beyond the effect on those concrete things of his own environment.

It is in this connection that what I have called the economic calculus proper helps us, at least by analogy, to see how this problem can be solved, and in fact is being solved, by the price system. Even the single controlling mind, in possession of all the data for some small, self-contained economic system, would not—every time some small adjustment in the allocation of resources had to be made—go explicitly through all the relations between ends and means which might possibly be affected. It is indeed the great contribution of the pure logic of choice that it has demonstrated conclusively that even such a single mind could solve this kind of problem only by constructing and constantly using rates of equivalence (or "values," or "marginal rates of substitution"), *i.e.*, by attaching to each kind of scarce resource a numerical index which cannot be derived from any property possessed by that particular thing, but which reflects, or in which is condensed, its significance in view of the whole means-end structure. In any small change he will have to consider only these quantitative indices (or "values") in which all the relevant information is concentrated; and by adjusting the quantities one by one, he can appropriately rearrange his dispositions without having to solve the whole puzzle *ab initio*, or without needing at any stage to survey it at once in all its ramifications.

Fundamentally, in a system in which the knowledge of the relevant facts is dispersed among many people, prices can act to coordinate the separate actions of different people in the same way as subjective values help the individual to coordinate the parts of his plan. It is worth contemplating for a moment a very simple and commonplace instance of the action of the price system to see what precisely it accomplishes. Assume that somewhere in the world a new opportunity for the use of some raw material, say tin, has arisen, or that one of the sources of supply of tin has been eliminated. It does not matter for our purpose—and it is very significant that it does not matter—which of these two causes has made tin more scarce. All that the users of tin need to know is that some of the tin they used to consume is now more profitably employed elsewhere, and that in consequence they must economize tin. There is no need for the great majority of them even to know where the more urgent need has arisen, or in favor of what other needs they ought to husband the supply. If only some of them know directly of the new demand, and switch resources over to it, and if the people who are aware of the new gap thus created in turn fill it from still other sources, the effect will rapidly spread throughout the whole economic system and influence not only all the uses of tin but also those of its substitutes and the substitutes of these substitutes, the supply of all the things made of tin, and their substitutes, and so on; and all this without the great majority of those instrumental in bringing about these substitutions knowing anything at all about the original cause of these changes. The whole acts as one market, not because any of its members survey the whole field, but because their limited individual fields of vision sufficiently overlap so that through many intermediaries the relevant information is communicated to all. The mere fact that there is one price for any commodity—or rather that local prices are connected in a manner determined by the cost of transport, etc.—brings about the solution which (it is just conceptually possible) might have been arrived at by one single mind possessing all the information which is in fact dispersed among all the people involved in the process.

VI

We must look at the price system as such a mechanism for communicating information if we want to understand its real function—a function which, of course, it fulfills less perfectly as prices grow more rigid. (Even when quoted prices have become quite rigid, however, the forces which would operate through changes in price still operate to a considerable extent through changes in the other terms of the contract.) The most significant fact about this system is the economy of knowledge with which it operates, or how little the individual participants need to know in order to be able to take the right action. In abbreviated form, by a kind of symbol, only the most essential information is passed on, and passed on only to those concerned. It is more than a metaphor to describe the price system as a kind of machinery for registering change, or a system of telecommunications which enables individual producers to watch merely the movement of a few pointers, as an engineer might watch the hands of a few dials, in order to adjust their activities to changes of which they may never know more than is reflected in the price movement.

Of course, these adjustments are probably never "perfect" in the sense in which the economist conceives of them in his equilibrium analysis. But I fear that our theoretical habit of approaching the problem with the assumption of more or less perfect knowledge on the part of almost everyone has made us somewhat blind to the true function of the price mechanism and led us to apply rather misleading standards in judging its efficiency. The marvel is that in a case like that of a scarcity of one raw material, without an order being issued, without more than perhaps a handful of people knowing the cause, tens of thousands of people whose identity could not be ascertained by months of investigation are made to use the material or its products more sparingly; *i.e.*, they move in the right direction. This is enough of a marvel even if, in a constantly changing world, not all will hit it off so perfectly that their profit rates will always be maintained at the same constant or "normal" level.

I have deliberately used the word "marvel" to shock the reader out of the complacency with which we often take the working of this mechanism for granted. I am convinced that if it were the result of deliberate human design, and if the people guided by the price changes understood that their decisions have significance far beyond their immediate aim, this mechanism would have been acclaimed as one of the greatest triumphs of the human mind. Its misfortune is the double one that it is not the product of human design and that the people guided by it usually do not know why they are made to do what they do. But those who clamor for "conscious direction"—and who cannot believe that anything which has evolved without design (and even without our understanding it) should solve problems which we should not be able to solve consciously—should remember this: The problem is precisely how to extend the span of our utilization of resources beyond the span of the control of any one mind; and, therefore, how to dispense with the need of conscious control and how to provide inducements which will make the individuals do the desirable things without anyone having to tell them what to do.

The problem which we meet here is by no means peculiar to economics but arises in connection with nearly all truly social phenomena, with language and with most of our cultural inheritance, and constitutes really the central theoretical problem of all social science. As Alfred Whitehead has said in another connection, "It is a profoundly erroneous truism, repeated by all copy-books and by eminent people when they are making speeches, that we should cultivate the habit of thinking what we are doing. The precise opposite is the case. Civilization advances by extending the number of important operations which we can perform without thinking about them." This is of profound significance in the social field. We make constant use of formulas, symbols, and rules whose meaning we do not understand and through the use of which we avail ourselves of the assistance of knowledge which individually we do not possess. We have developed these practices and institutions by building upon habits and institutions which have proved successful in their own sphere and which have in turn become the foundation of the civilization we have built up.

The price system is just one of those formations which man has learned to use (though he is still very far from having learned to make the best use of it) after he had stumbled upon it without understanding it. Through it not only a division of labor but also a coordinated utilization of resources based on an equally divided knowledge has become possible. The people who like to deride any suggestion that this may be so usually distort the argument by insinuating that it asserts that by some miracle just that sort of system has spontaneously grown up which is best suited to modern civilization. It is the other way round: man has been able to develop that division of labor on which our civilization is based because he happened to stumble upon a method which made it possible. Had he not done so he might still have developed some other, altogether different, type of civilization, something like the "state" of the termite ants, or some other altogether unimaginable type. All that we can say is that nobody has yet succeeded in designing an alternative system in which certain features of the existing one can be preserved which are dear even to those who most violently assail it—such as particularly the extent to which the individual can choose his pursuits and consequently freely use his own knowledge and skill.

VII

It is in many ways fortunate that the dispute about the indispensability of the price system for any rational calculation in a complex society is now no longer conducted entirely between camps holding different political views. The thesis that without the price system we could not preserve a society based on such extensive division of labor as ours was greeted with a howl of derision when it was first advanced by von Mises twenty-five years ago. Today the difficulties which some still find in accepting it are no longer mainly political, and this makes for an atmosphere much more conducive to reasonable discussion. When we find Leon Trotsky arguing that "economic accounting is unthinkable without market relations"; when Professor Oscar Lange promises Professor von Mises a statue in the marble halls of the future Central Planning Board; and when Professor Abba P. Lerner rediscovers Adam Smith and emphasizes that the essential utility of the price system consists in inducing the individual, while seeking his own interest, to do what is in the general interest, the differences can indeed no longer be ascribed to political prejudice. The remaining dissent seems clearly to be due to purely intellectual, and more particularly methodological, differences.

A recent statement by Professor Joseph Schumpeter in his *Capitalism, Socialism and Democracy* provides a clear illustration of one of the methodological differences which I have in mind. Its author is pre-eminent among those economists who approach economic phenomena in the light of a certain branch of positivism. To him these phenomena accordingly appear as objectively given quantities of commodities impinging directly upon each other, almost, it would seem, without any intervention of human minds. Only against this background can I account for the following (to me startling) pronouncement. Professor Schumpeter argues that the possibility of a rational calculation in the absence of markets for the factors of production follows for the theorist "from the elementary proposition that consumers in evaluating ('demanding') consumers' goods *ipso facto* also evaluate the means of production which enter into the production of these goods."[1]

[1]J. Schumpeter, *Capitalism, Socialism and Democracy* (New York; Harper, 1942), p. 175. Professor Schumpeter is, I believe, also the original author of the myth that Pareto and Barone have "solved" the problem of socialist calculation. What they, and many others, did was merely to state the conditions which a rational allocation of resources would have to satisfy and to point out that these were essentially the same as the conditions of equilibrium of a competitive market. This is something altogether different from showing how the allocation of resources satisfying these conditions can be found in practice. Pareto himself (from whom Barone has taken practically everything he has to say), far from claiming to have solved the practical problem, in fact explicitly denies that it can be solved without the help of the market. See his *Manuel d'économie pure* (2nd ed., 1927), pp. 233–34. The relevant passage is quoted in an English translation at the beginning of my article on "Socialist Calculation: The Competitive 'Solution,'" in *Economica*, New Series, Vol. VIII, No. 26 (May, 1940), p. 125.

Taken literally, this statement is simply untrue. The consumers do nothing of the kind. What Professor Schumpeter's "*ipso facto*" presumably means is that the valuation of the factors of production is implied in, or follows necessarily from, the valuation of consumers' goods. But this, too, is not correct. Implication is a logical relationship which can be meaningfully asserted only of propositions simultaneously present to one and the same mind. It is evident, however, that the values of the factors of production do not depend solely on the valuation of the consumers' goods but also on the conditions of supply of the various factors of production. Only to a mind to which all these facts were simultaneously known would the answer necessarily follow from the facts given to it. The practical problem, however, arises precisely because these facts are never so given to a single mind, and because, in consequence, it is necessary that in the solution of the problem knowledge should be used that is dispersed among many people.

The problem is thus in no way solved if we can show that all the facts, *if* they were known to a single mind (as we hypothetically assume them to be given to the observing economist), would uniquely determine the solution; instead we must show how a solution is produced by the interactions of people each of whom possesses only partial knowledge. To assume all the knowledge to be given to a single mind in the same manner in which we assume it to be given to us as the explaining economists is to assume the problem away and to disregard everything that is important and significant in the real world.

That an economist of Professor Schumpeter's standing should thus have fallen into a trap which the ambiguity of the term "datum" sets to the unwary can hardly be explained as a simple error. It suggests rather that there is something fundamentally wrong with an approach which habitually disregards an essential part of the phenomena with which we have to deal: the unavoidable imperfection of man's knowledge and the consequent need for a process by which knowledge is constantly communicated and acquired. Any approach, such as that of much of mathematical economics with its simultaneous equations, which in effect starts from the assumption that people's *knowledge* corresponds with the objective *facts* of the situation, systematically leaves out what is our main task to explain. I am far from denying that in our system equilibrium analysis has a useful function to perform. But when it comes to the point where it misleads some of our leading thinkers into believing that the situation which it describes has direct relevance to the solution of practical problems, it is high time that we remember that it does not deal with the social process at all and that it is no more than a useful preliminary to the study of the main problem.

Chapter 4

The Meaning of Competition*

I

There are signs of increasing awareness among economists that what they have been discussing in recent years under the name of "competition" is not the same thing as what is thus called in ordinary language. But, although there have been some valiant attempts to bring discussion back to earth and to direct attention to the problems of real life, notably by J. M. Clark and F. Machlup,[1] the general view seems still to regard the conception of competition currently employed by economists as the significant one and to treat that of the businessman as an abuse. It appears to be generally held that the so-called theory of "perfect competition" provides the appropriate model for judging the effectiveness of competition in real life and

*This text is based on the version of this essay published as chapter 5 of *Individualism and Economic Order* (University of Chicago Press, 1948). It reproduces the substance of the Stafford Little Lecture delivered at Princeton University on May 20, 1946.

[1]J. M. Clark, "Toward a Concept of Workable Competition," *American Economic Review*, Vol. XXX (June, 1940); F. Machlup, "Competition, Oligopoly, and Profit," *Economica*, Vol. IX (new ser.; February and May, 1942).

that, to the extent that real competition differs from that model, it is undesirable and even harmful.

For this attitude there seems to me to exist very little justification. I shall attempt to show that what the theory of perfect competition discusses has little claim to be called "competition" at all and that its conclusions are of little use as guides to policy. The reason for this seems to me to be that this theory throughout assumes that state of affairs already to exist which, according to the truer view of the older theory, the process of competition tends to bring about (or to approximate) and that, if the state of affairs assumed by the theory of perfect competition ever existed, it would not only deprive of their scope all the activities which the verb "to compete" describes but would make them virtually impossible.

If all this affected only the use of the word "competition," it would not matter a great deal. But it seems almost as if economists by this peculiar use of language were deceiving themselves into the belief that, in discussing "competition," they are saying something about the nature and significance of the process by which the state of affairs is brought about which they merely assume to exist. In fact, this moving force of economic life is left almost altogether undiscussed.

I do not wish to discuss here at any length the reasons which have led the theory of competition into this curious state. As I have suggested elsewhere in this volume,[2] the tautological method which is appropriate and indispensable for the analysis of individual action seems in this instance to have been illegitimately extended to problems in which we have to deal with a social process in which the decisions of many individuals influence one another

---

[2]See the second and fourth chapters [of *Individualism and Economic Order* (Chicago: University of Chicago Press, 1948)].

and necessarily succeed one another in time. The economic calculus (or the Pure Logic of Choice) which deals with the first kind of problem consists of an apparatus of classification of possible human attitudes and provides us with a technique for describing the interrelations of the different parts of a single plan. Its conclusions are implicit in its assumptions: the desires and the knowledge of the facts, which are assumed to be simultaneously present to a single mind, determine a unique solution. The relations discussed in this type of analysis are logical relations, concerned solely with the conclusions which follow for the mind of the planning individual from the given premises.

When we deal, however, with a situation in which a number of persons are attempting to work out their separate plans, we can no longer assume that the data are the same for all the planning minds. The problem becomes one of how the "data" of the different individuals on which they base their plans are adjusted to the objective facts of their environment (which includes the actions of the other people). Although in the solution of this type of problem we still must make use of our technique for rapidly working out the implications of a given set of data, we have now to deal not only with several separate sets of data of the different persons but also—and this is even more important—with a process which necessarily involves continuous changes in the data for the different individuals. As I have suggested before, the causal factor enters here in the form of the acquisition of new knowledge by the different individuals or of changes in their data brought about by the contacts between them.

The relevance of this for my present problem will appear when it is recalled that the modern theory of competition deals almost exclusively with a state of what is called "competitive equilibrium" in which it is assumed that the data for the different individuals are fully adjusted to each other, while the problem which requires explanation is the nature of the process by which the data are thus adjusted. In other words, the description of competitive equilibrium does not even attempt to say that, if we find such and such conditions, such and such consequences will follow, but confines itself to defining conditions in which its conclusions are already implicitly contained and which may conceivably exist but of which it does not tell us how they can ever be brought about. Or, to anticipate our main conclusion in a brief statement, competition is by its nature a dynamic process whose essential characteristics are assumed away by the assumptions underlying static analysis.

II

That the modern theory of competitive equilibrium *assumes* the situation to exist which a true explanation ought to account for as the effect of the competitive process is best shown by examining the familiar list of conditions found in any modern textbook. Most of these conditions, incidentally, not only underlie the analysis of "perfect" competition but are equally assumed in the discussion of the various "imperfect" or "monopolistic" markets, which throughout assume certain unrealistic "perfections."[3] For our immediate purpose, however, the theory of perfect competition will be the most instructive case to examine.

While different authors may state the list of essential conditions of perfect competition differently, the following is probably more than sufficiently comprehensive for our purpose, because, as we shall see, those conditions are not really independent of each other. According to

[3]Particularly the assumptions that *at all times* a uniform price must rule for a given commodity throughout the market and that sellers know the shape of the demand curve.

the generally accepted view, perfect competition presupposes:

1. A homogeneous commodity offered and demanded by a large number of relatively small sellers or buyers, none of whom expects to exercise by his action a perceptible influence on price.

2. Free entry into the market and absence of other restraints on the movement of prices and resources.

3. Complete knowledge of the relevant factors on the part of all participants in the market.

We shall not ask at this stage precisely for what these conditions are required or what is implied if they are assumed to be given. But we must inquire a little further about their meaning, and in this respect it is the third condition which is the critical and obscure one. The standard can evidently not be perfect knowledge of everything affecting the market on the part of every person taking part in it. I shall here not go into the familiar paradox of the paralyzing effect really perfect knowledge and foresight would have on all action.[4] It will be obvious also that nothing is solved when we assume everybody to know everything and that the real problem is rather how it can be brought about that as much of the available knowledge as possible is used. This raises for a competitive society the question, not how we can "find" the people who know best, but rather what institutional arrangements are necessary in order that the unknown persons who have knowledge specially suited to a particular task are most likely to be attracted to that task. But we must inquire a little further what sort of knowledge it is that is supposed to be in possession of the parties of the market.

---

[4]See O. Morgenstern, "Vollkommene Voraussicht und wirtschaftliches Gleichgewicht," *Zeitschrift für Nationalökonomie*, Vol. VI (1935).

If we consider the market for some kind of finished consumption goods and start with the position of its producers or sellers, we shall find, first, that they are assumed to know the lowest cost at which the commodity can be produced. Yet this knowledge which is assumed to be given to begin with is one of the main points where it is only through the process of competition that the facts will be discovered. This appears to me one of the most important of the points where the starting point of the theory of competitive equilibrium assumes away the main task which only the process of competition can solve. The position is somewhat similar with respect to the second point on which the producers are assumed to be fully informed: the wishes and desires of the consumers, including the kinds of goods and services which they demand and the prices they are willing to pay. These cannot properly be regarded as given facts but ought rather to be regarded as problems to be solved by the process of competition.

The same situation exists on the side of the consumers or buyers. Again the knowledge they are supposed to possess in a state of competitive equilibrium cannot be legitimately assumed to be at their command before the process of competition starts. Their knowledge of the alternatives before them is the result of what happens on the market, of such activities as advertising, etc.; and the whole organization of the market serves mainly the need of spreading the information on which the buyer is to act.

The peculiar nature of the assumptions from which the theory of competitive equilibrium starts stands out very clearly if we ask which of the activities that are commonly designated by the verb "to compete" would still be possible if those conditions were all satisfied. Perhaps it is worth recalling that, according to Dr. Johnson, competition is "the act of endeavouring to gain what another endeavours to gain at the same time." Now, how many of the devices adopted in ordinary life to that end would still be open to a seller in a market in which so-called "perfect competition" prevails? I believe that the answer is exactly none. Advertising, undercutting, and improving ("differentiating") the goods or services produced are all excluded by definition—"perfect" competition means indeed the absence of all competitive activities.

Especially remarkable in this connection is the explicit and complete exclusion from the theory of perfect competition of all personal relationships existing between the parties.[5] In actual life the fact that our inadequate knowledge of the available commodities or services is made up for by our experience with the persons or firms supplying them—that competition is in a large measure competition for reputation or good will—is one of the most important facts which enables us to solve our daily problems. The function of competition is here precisely to teach us *who* will serve us well: which grocer or travel agency, which department store or hotel, which doctor or solicitor we can expect to provide the most satisfactory solution for whatever particular personal problem we may have to face. Evidently in all these fields competition may be very intense, just because the services of the different persons or firms will never be exactly alike, and it will be owing to this competition that we are in a position to be served as well as we are. The reasons competition in this field is described as imperfect have indeed nothing to do with the competitive character of the activities of these people; they lie in the nature of the commodities or services themselves. If no two doctors are perfectly alike, this does not mean that the competition between them is less intense but merely that any degree of competition between them

---

[5]Cf. G. J. Stigler, *The Theory of Price* (1946), p. 24: "Economic relationships are never perfectly competitive if they involve any personal relationships between economic units" (see also *ibid.*, p. 226).

will not produce exactly those results which it would if their services were exactly alike. This is not a purely verbal point. The talk about the defects of competition when we are in fact talking about the necessary difference between commodities and services conceals a very real confusion and leads on occasion to absurd conclusions.

While on a first glance the assumption concerning the perfect knowledge possessed by the parties may seem the most startling and artificial of all those on which the theory of perfect competition is based, it may in fact be no more than a consequence of, and in part even justified by, another of the presuppositions on which it is founded. If, indeed, we start by assuming that a large number of people are producing the same commodity and command the same objective facilities and opportunities for doing so, then indeed it might be made plausible (although this has, to my knowledge, never been attempted) that they will in time all be led to know most of the facts relevant for judging the market of that commodity. Not only will each producer by his experience learn the same facts as every other but also he will thus come to know what his fellows know and in consequence the elasticity of the demand for his own product. The condition where different manufacturers produce the identical product under identical conditions is in fact the most favorable for producing that state of knowledge among them which perfect competition requires. Perhaps this means no more than that the commodities can be identical in the sense in which it is alone relevant for our understanding human action only if people hold the same views about them, although it should also be possible to state a set of physical conditions which is favorable to all those who are concerned with a set of closely interrelated activities learning the facts relevant for their decisions.

However that be, it will be clear that the facts will not always be as favorable to this result as they are when many people are at least in a position to produce the same article. The conception of the economic system as divisible into distinct markets for separate commodities is after all very largely the product of the imagination of the economist and certainly is not the rule in the field of manufacture and of personal services, to which the discussion about competition so largely refers. In fact, it need hardly be said, no products of two producers are ever exactly alike, even if it were only because, as they leave his plant, they must be at different places. These differences are part of the facts which create our economic problem, and it is little help to answer it on the assumption that they are absent.

The belief in the advantages of perfect competition frequently leads enthusiasts even to argue that a more advantageous use of resources would be achieved if the existing variety of products were reduced by *compulsory* standardization. Now, there is undoubtedly much to be said in many fields for assisting standardization by agreed recommendations or standards which are to apply unless different requirements are explicitly stipulated in contracts. But this is something very different from the demands of those who believe that the variety of people's tastes should be disregarded and the constant experimentation with improvements should be suppressed in order to obtain the advantages of perfect competition. It would clearly not be an improvement to build all houses exactly alike in order to create a perfect market for houses, and the same is true of most other fields where differences between the individual products prevent competition from ever being perfect.

III

We shall probably learn more about the nature and significance of the competitive process if for a while we forget about the artificial assumptions underlying the theory of perfect competition and ask whether competition would be any less important if, for example, no two commodities were ever exactly alike. If it were not for the difficulty of the analysis of such a situation, it would be well worth while to consider in some detail the case where the different commodities could not be readily classed into distinct groups, but where we had to deal with a continuous range of close substitutes, every unit somewhat different from the other but without any marked break in the continuous range. The result of the analysis of competition in such a situation might in many respects be more relevant to the conditions of real life than those of the analysis of competition in a single industry producing a homogeneous commodity sharply differentiated from all others. Or, if the case where no two commodities are exactly alike be thought to be too extreme, we might at least turn to the case where no two producers produce exactly the same commodity, as is the rule not only with all personal services but also in the markets of many manufactured commodities, such as the markets for books or musical instruments.

For our present purpose I need not attempt anything like a complete analysis of such kinds of markets but shall merely ask what would be the role of competition in them. Although the result would, of course, within fairly wide margins be indeterminate, the market would still bring about a set of prices at which each commodity sold just cheap enough to outbid its potential close substitutes—and this in itself is no small thing when we consider the unsurmountable difficulties of discovering even such a system of prices by any other method except that of trial and error in the market, with the individual participants gradually learning the relevant circumstances. It is true, of course, that in such a market correspondence between prices and marginal costs is to be expected only to the degree that elasticities of demand for the individual commodities approach the conditions assumed by the theory of perfect competition or that elasticities of substitution between the different commodities approach infinity. But the point is that in this case this standard of perfection as something desirable or to be aimed at is wholly irrelevant. The basis of comparison, on the grounds of which the achievement of competition ought to be judged, cannot be a situation which is different from the objective facts and which cannot be brought about by any known means. It ought to be the situation as it would exist if competition were prevented from operating. Not the approach to an unachievable and meaningless ideal but the improvement upon the conditions that would exist without competition should be the test.

In such a situation how would conditions differ, if competition were "free" in the traditional sense, from those which would exist if, for example, only people licensed by authority were allowed to produce particular things, or prices were fixed by authority, or both? Clearly there would be not only no likelihood that the different things would be produced by those who knew best how to do it and therefore could do it at lowest cost but also no likelihood that all those things would be produced at all which, if the consumers had the choice, they would like best. There would be little relationship between actual prices and the lowest cost at which somebody would be able to produce these commodities; indeed, the alternatives between which both producers and consumers would be in a position to choose, their data, would be altogether different from what they would be under competition.

The real problem in all this is not whether we will get *given* commodities or services at *given* marginal costs but mainly by what commodities and services the needs of the people can be most cheaply satisfied. The solution of the economic problem of society is in this respect always a voyage of exploration into the unknown, an attempt to discover new ways of doing things better than they have been done before. This must always remain so as long as there are any economic problems to be solved at all, because all economic problems are created by unforeseen changes which require adaptation. Only what we have not foreseen and provided for requires new decisions. If no such adaptations were required, if at any moment we knew that all change had stopped and things would forever go on exactly as they are now, there would be no more questions of the use of resources to be solved.

A person who possesses the exclusive knowledge or skill which enables him to reduce the cost of production of a commodity by 50 percent still renders an enormous service to society if he enters its production and reduces its price by only 25 percent—not only through that price reduction but also through his additional saving of cost. But it is only through competition that we can assume that these possible savings of cost will be achieved. Even if in each instance prices were only just low enough to keep out producers which do not enjoy these or other equivalent advantages, so that each commodity were produced as cheaply as possible, though many may be sold at prices considerably above costs, this would probably be a result which could not be achieved by any other method than that of letting competition operate.

IV

That in conditions of real life the position even of any two producers is hardly ever the same is due to facts which the theory of perfect competition eliminates by its concentration on a long-term equilibrium which in an ever changing world can never be reached. At any given moment the equipment of a particular firm is always largely determined by historical accident, and the problem is that it should make the best use of the given equipment (including the acquired capacities of the members of its staff) and not what it should do if it were given unlimited time to adjust itself to constant conditions. For the problem of the best use of the given durable but exhaustible resources the long-term equilibrium price with which a theory discussing "perfect" competition must be concerned is not only not relevant; the conclusions concerning policy to which preoccupation with this model leads are highly misleading and even dangerous. The idea that under "perfect" competition prices should be equal to long-run costs often leads to the approval of such antisocial practices as the demand for an "orderly competition" which will secure a fair return on capital and for the destruction of excess capacity. Enthusiasm for perfect competition in theory and the support of monopoly in practice are indeed surprisingly often found to live together.

This is, however, only one of the many points on which the neglect of the time element makes the theoretical picture of perfect competition so entirely remote from all that is relevant to an understanding of the process of competition. If we think of it, as we ought to, as a succession of events, it becomes even more obvious that in real life there will at any moment be as a rule only one producer who can manufacture a given article at the lowest cost and who may in fact sell below the cost of his next successful competitor, but who, while still trying to extend his market, will often be overtaken by somebody else, who in turn will be prevented from capturing the whole market by yet another, and so on. Such a market would clearly never be in a state of perfect competition, yet competition in it might not only be as intense as possible but would also be the essential factor in bringing about the fact that the article in question is supplied at any moment to the consumer as cheaply as this can be done by any known method.

When we compare an "imperfect" market like this with a relatively "perfect" market as that of, say, grain, we shall now be in a better position to bring out the distinction which has been underlying this whole discussion—the distinction between the underlying objective facts of a situation which cannot be altered by human activity and the nature of the competitive activities by which men adjust themselves to the situation. Where, as in the latter case, we have a highly organized market of a fully standardized commodity produced by many producers, there is little need or scope for competitive activities because the situation is such that the conditions which these activities might bring about are already satisfied to begin with. The best ways of producing the commodity, its character and uses, are most of the time known to nearly the same degree to all members of the market. The knowledge of any important change spreads so rapidly and the adaptation to it is so soon effected that we usually simply disregard what happens during these short transition periods and confine ourselves to comparing the two states of near-equilibrium which exist before and after them. But it is during this short and neglected interval that the forces of competition operate and become visible, and it is the events during this interval which we must study if we are to "explain" the equilibrium which follows it.

It is only in a market where adaptation is slow compared with the rate of change that the process of competition is in continuous operation. And though the reason why adaptation is slow *may* be that competition is weak, e.g., because there are special obstacles to entry into the trade, or because of some other factors of the character of natural monopolies, slow adaptation does by no means necessarily mean weak competition. When the variety of near-substitutes is great and rapidly changing, where it takes a long time to find out about the relative merits of the available alternatives, or where the need for a whole class of goods or services occurs only discontinuously at irregular intervals, the adjustment must be slow even if competition is strong and active.

The confusion between the objective facts of the situation and the character of the human responses to it tends to conceal from us the important fact that competition is the more important the more complex or "imperfect" are the objective conditions in which it has to operate. Indeed, far from competition being beneficial only when it is "perfect," I am inclined to argue that the need for competition is nowhere greater than in fields in which the nature of the commodities or services makes it impossible that it ever should create a perfect market in the theoretical sense. The inevitable actual imperfections of competition are as little an argument against competition as the difficulties of achieving a perfect solution of any other task are an argument against attempting to solve it at all, or as little as imperfect health is an argument against health.

In conditions where we can never have many people offering the same homogeneous product or service, because of the ever changing character of our needs and our knowledge, or of the infinite variety of human skills and capacities, the ideal state cannot be one requiring an identical character of large numbers of such products and services. The economic problem is a problem of making the best use of what resources we have, and not one of what we should do if the situation were different from what it actually is. There is no sense in talking of a use of resources "as if" a perfect market existed, if this means that the resources would have to be different from what they are, or in discussing what somebody with perfect knowledge would do if our task must be to make the best use of the knowledge the existing people have.

V

The argument in favor of competition does not rest on the conditions that would exist if it were perfect. Although, where the objective facts would make it possible for competition to approach perfection, this would also secure the most effective use of resources, and, although there is therefore every case for removing human obstacles to competition, this does not mean that competition does not also bring about as effective a use of resources as can be brought about by any known means where in the nature of the case it must be imperfect. Even where free entry will secure no more than that at any one moment all the goods and services for which there would be an effective demand if they were available are in fact produced at the least current[6] expenditure of resources at which, in the given historical situation, they can be produced, even though the price the consumer is made to pay for them is considerably higher and only just below the cost of the next best way in which his need could be satisfied, this, I submit, is more than we can expect from any other known system. The decisive point is still the elementary one that it is most unlikely that, without artificial obstacles which government activity either creates or can remove, any commodity or service will for any length of time be available only at a price at which outsiders could expect a more than normal profit if they entered the field.

The practical lesson of all this, I think, is that we should worry much less about whether competition in a given case is perfect and worry much more about whether there is competition at all. What our theoretical models of separate industries conceal is that in practice a much

[6]"Current" cost in this connection excludes all true bygones but includes, of course, "user cost."

bigger gulf divides competition from no competition than perfect from imperfect competition. Yet the current tendency in discussion is to be intolerant about the imperfections and to be silent about the prevention of competition. We can probably still learn more about the real significance of competition by studying the results which regularly occur where competition is deliberately suppressed than by concentrating on the shortcomings of actual competition compared with an ideal which is irrelevant for the given facts. I say advisedly "where competition is deliberately suppressed" and not merely "where it is absent," because its main effects are usually operating, even if more slowly, so long as it is not outright suppressed with the assistance or the tolerance of the state. The evils which experience has shown to be the regular consequence of a suppression of competition are on a different plane from those which the imperfections of competition may cause. Much more serious than the fact that prices may not correspond to marginal cost is the fact that, with an entrenched monopoly, costs are likely to be much higher than is necessary. A monopoly based on superior efficiency, on the other hand, does comparatively little harm so long as it is assured that it will disappear as soon as anyone else becomes more efficient in providing satisfaction to the consumers.

In conclusion I want for a moment to go back to the point from which I started and restate the most important conclusion in a more general form. Competition is essentially a process of the formation of opinion: by spreading information, it creates that unity and coherence of the economic system which we presuppose when we think of it as one market. It creates the views people have about what is best and cheapest, and it is because of it that people know at least as much about possibilities and opportunities as they in fact do. It is thus a process which involves a continuous change in the data and whose significance must therefore be completely missed by any theory which treats these data as constant.

CHAPTER 5

The *Non Sequitur* of the "Dependence Effect"*

For well over a hundred years the critics of the free enterprise system have resorted to the argument that if production were only organized rationally, there would be no economic problem. Rather than face the problem which scarcity creates, socialist reformers have tended to deny that scarcity existed. Ever since the Saint-Simonians their contention has been that the problem of production has been solved and only the problem of distribution remains. However absurd this contention must appear to us with respect to the time when it was first advanced, it still has some persuasive power when repeated with reference to the present.

The latest form of this old contention is expounded in *The Affluent Society* by Professor J. K. Galbraith. He attempts to demonstrate that in our affluent society the important private needs are already satisfied and the urgent need is therefore no longer a further expansion of the output of commodities but an increase of those services which are supplied (and presumably can be supplied only) by government. Though this book

*This text is based on the version of this essay published in the *Southern Economic Journal* 27, no. 4 (1961): 346–48.

has been extensively discussed since its publication in 1958, its central thesis still requires some further examination.

I believe the author would agree that his argument turns upon the "Dependence Effect" explained in chapter XI of the book. The argument of this chapter starts from the assertion that a great part of the wants which are still unsatisfied in modern society are not wants which would be experienced spontaneously by the individual if left to himself, but are wants which are created by the process by which they are satisfied. It is then represented as self-evident that for this reason such wants cannot be urgent or important. This crucial conclusion appears to be a complete *non sequitur* and it would seem that with it the whole argument of the book collapses.

The first part of the argument is of course perfectly true: we would not desire any of the amenities of civilization—or even of the most primitive culture—if we did not live in a society in which others provide them. The innate wants are probably confined to food, shelter, and sex. All the rest we learn to desire because we see others enjoying various things. To say that a desire is not important because it is not innate is to say that the whole cultural achievement of man is not important.

This cultural origin of practically all the needs of civilized life must of course not be confused with the fact that there are some desires which aim, not at a satisfaction derived directly from the use of an object, but only from the status which its consumption is expected to confer. In a passage which Professor Galbraith quotes (p. 118), Lord Keynes seems to treat the latter sort of Veblenesque conspicuous consumption as the only alternative "to those needs which are absolute in the sense that we feel them whatever the situation of our fellow human beings may be." If the latter phrase is interpreted to exclude all the needs for goods which are felt only because these goods are known to be produced, these two Keynesian classes describe of course only extreme types of wants, but disregard the overwhelming majority of goods on which civilized life rests. Very few needs indeed are "absolute" in the sense that they are independent of social environment or of the example of others, and that their satisfaction is an indispensable condition for the preservation of the individual or of the species. Most needs which make us act are needs for things which only civilization teaches us exist at all, and these things are wanted by us because they produce feelings or emotions which we would not know if it were not for our cultural inheritance. Are not in this sense probably all our esthetic feelings "acquired tastes"?

How complete a *non sequitur* Professor Galbraith's conclusion represents is seen most clearly if we apply the argument to any product of the arts, be it music, painting, or literature. If the fact that people would not feel the need for something if it were not produced did prove that such products are of small value, all those highest products of human endeavor would be of small value. Professor Galbraith's argument could be easily employed, without any change of the essential terms, to demonstrate the worthlessness of literature or any other form of art. Surely an individual's want for literature is not original with himself in the sense that he would experience it if literature were not produced. Does this then mean that the production of literature cannot be defended as satisfying a want because it is only the production which provokes the demand? In this, as in the case of all cultural needs, it is unquestionably, in Professor Galbraith's words, "the process of satisfying the wants that creates the wants." There have never been "independently determined desires for" literature before literature has been produced and books certainly do not serve the "simple mode of enjoyment which requires no previous conditioning of the consumer" (p. 217). Clearly my taste for the novels of Jane Austen or Anthony Trollope or C. P. Snow is not "original with myself." But is it not rather absurd to conclude from this that it is less important than, say, the need for education? Public education indeed seems to regard it as one of its tasks to instill a taste for literature in the young and even employs producers of literature for that purpose. Is this want creation by the producer reprehensible? Or does the fact that some of the pupils may possess a taste for poetry only because of the efforts of their teachers prove that since "it does not arise in spontaneous consumer need and the demand would not exist were it not contrived, its utility or urgency, ex contrivance, is zero"?

The appearance that the conclusions follow from the admitted facts is made possible by an obscurity of the wording of the argument with respect to which it is difficult to know whether the author is himself the victim of a confusion or whether he skillfully uses ambiguous terms to make the conclusion appear plausible. The obscurity concerns the implied assertion that the wants of consumers are determined by the producers. Professor Galbraith avoids in this connection any terms as crude and definite as "determine." The expressions he employs, such as that wants are "dependent on" or the "fruits of" production, or that "production creates the wants" do, of course, suggest determination but avoid saying so in plain terms. After what has already been said it is of course obvious that the knowledge of what is being produced is one of the many factors on which depends what people will want. It would scarcely be an exaggeration to say that contemporary man, in all fields where he has not yet formed firm habits, tends to find out what he wants by looking at what his neighbors do and at various displays of goods (physical or in catalogues or advertisements) and then choosing what he likes best.

In this sense the tastes of man, as is also true of his opinions and beliefs and indeed much of his personality, are shaped in a great measure by his cultural environment. But though in some contexts it would perhaps be legitimate to express this by a phrase like "production creates the wants," the circumstances mentioned would clearly not justify the contention that particular producers can deliberately determine the wants of particular consumers. The efforts of all producers will certainly be directed towards that end; but how far any individual producer will succeed will depend not only on what he does but also on what the others do and on a great many other influences operating upon the consumer. The joint but uncoordinated efforts of the producers merely create one element of the environment by which the wants of the consumers are shaped. It is because each individual producer thinks that the consumers can be persuaded to like his products that he endeavors to influence them. But though this effort is part of the influences which shape consumers' tastes, no producer can in any real sense "determine" them. This, however, is clearly implied in such statements as that wants are "both passively and deliberately the fruits of the process by which they are satisfied" (p. 124). If the producer could in fact deliberately determine what the consumers will want, Professor Galbraith's conclusions would have some validity. But though this is skillfully suggested, it is nowhere made credible, and could hardly be made credible because it is not true. Though the range of choice open to the consumers is the joint result of, among other things, the efforts of all producers who vie with each other in making their respective products appear more attractive than those of their competitors, every particular consumer still has the choice between all those different offers.

A fuller examination of this process would, of course, have to consider how, after the efforts of some producers have actually swayed some consumers, it becomes the example of the various consumers thus persuaded which will influence the remaining consumers. This can be mentioned here only to emphasize that even if each consumer were exposed to pressure of only one producer, the harmful effects which are apprehended from this would soon be offset by the much more powerful example of his fellows. It is of course fashionable to treat this influence of the example of others (or, what comes to the same thing, the learning from the experience made by others) as if it amounted all to an attempt of keeping up with the Joneses and for that reason was to be regarded as detrimental. It seems to me not only that the importance of this factor is usually greatly exaggerated but also that it is not really relevant to Professor Galbraith's main thesis. But it might be worthwhile briefly to ask what, assuming that some expenditure were actually determined solely by a desire of keeping up with the Joneses, that would really prove? At least in Europe we used to be familiar with a type of persons who often denied themselves even enough food in order to maintain an appearance of respectability or gentility in dress and style of life. We may regard this as a misguided effort, but surely it would not prove that the income of such persons was larger than they knew how to use wisely. That the appearance of success, or wealth, may to some people seem more important than many other needs does in no way prove that the needs they sacrifice to the former are unimportant. In the same way, even though people are often persuaded to spend unwisely, this surely is no evidence that they do not still have important unsatisfied needs.

Professor Galbraith's attempt to give an apparent scientific proof for the contention that the need for the production of more commodities has greatly decreased seems to me to have broken down completely. With it goes the claim to have produced a valid argument which justifies the use of coercion to make people employ their income for those purposes of which he approves. It is not to be denied that there is some originality in this latest version of the old socialist argument. For over a hundred years we have been exhorted to embrace socialism because it would give us more goods. Since it has so lamentably failed to achieve this where it has been tried, we are now urged to adopt it because more goods after all are not important. The aim is still progressively to increase the share of the resources whose use is determined by political authority and the coercion of any dissenting minority. It is not surprising, therefore, that Professor Galbraith's thesis has been most enthusiastically received by the intellectuals of the British Labour Party, where his influence bids fair to displace that of the late Lord Keynes. It is more curious that in this country it is not recognized as an outright socialist argument and often seems to appeal to people on the opposite end of the political spectrum. But this is probably only another instance of the familiar fact that on these matters the extremes frequently meet.

Chapter 6

The Pretense of Knowledge*

The particular occasion of this lecture, combined with the chief practical problem which economists have to face today, have made the choice of its topic almost inevitable. On the one hand the still recent establishment of the Nobel Memorial Prize in Economic Science marks a significant step in the process by which, in the opinion of the general public, economics has been conceded some of the dignity and prestige of the physical sciences. On the other hand, the economists are at this moment called upon to say how to extricate the free world from the serious threat of accelerating inflation which, it must be admitted, has been brought about by policies which the majority of economists recommended and even urged governments to pursue. We have indeed at the moment little cause for pride: as a profession we have made a mess of things.

It seems to me that this failure of the economists to guide policy more successfully is closely connected with their propensity to imitate as closely as possible the procedures of the brilliantly successful physical sciences—an

*This text is based on Hayek's Prize Lecture delivered at the ceremony awarding him the Nobel Prize in economics on December 11, 1974, in Stockholm, Sweden.

attempt which in our field may lead to outright error. It is an approach which has come to be described as the "scientistic" attitude—an attitude which, as I defined it some thirty years ago, "is decidedly unscientific in the true sense of the word, since it involves a mechanical and uncritical application of habits of thought to fields different from those in which they have been formed."[1] I want today to begin by explaining how some of the gravest errors of recent economic policy are a direct consequence of this scientistic error.

The theory which has been guiding monetary and financial policy during the last thirty years, and which I contend is largely the product of such a mistaken conception of the proper scientific procedure, consists in the assertion that there exists a simple positive correlation between total employment and the size of the aggregate demand for goods and services; it leads to the belief that we can permanently assure full employment by maintaining total money expenditure at an appropriate level. Among the various theories advanced to account for extensive unemployment, this is probably the only one in support of which strong quantitative evidence can be adduced. I nevertheless regard it as fundamentally false, and to act upon it, as we now experience, as very harmful.

This brings me to the crucial issue. Unlike the position that exists in the physical sciences, in economics and other disciplines that deal with essentially complex phenomena, the aspects of the events to be accounted for about which we can get quantitative data are necessarily limited and may not include the important ones. While in the physical sciences it is generally assumed, probably

[1]"Scientism and the Study of Society," *Economica*, vol. IX, no. 35, August 1942, reprinted in *The Counter-Revolution of Science*, Glencoe, Ill., 1952, p. 15 of this reprint.

with good reason, that any important factor which determines the observed events will itself be directly observable and measurable, in the study of such complex phenomena as the market, which depend on the actions of many individuals, all the circumstances which will determine the outcome of a process, for reasons which I shall explain later, will hardly ever be fully known or measurable. And while in the physical sciences the investigator will be able to measure what, on the basis of a *prima facie* theory, he thinks important, in the social sciences often that is treated as important which happens to be accessible to measurement. This is sometimes carried to the point where it is demanded that our theories must be formulated in such terms that they refer only to measurable magnitudes.

It can hardly be denied that such a demand quite arbitrarily limits the facts which are to be admitted as possible causes of the events which occur in the real world. This view, which is often quite naively accepted as required by scientific procedure, has some rather paradoxical consequences. We know, of course, with regard to the market and similar social structures, a great many facts which we cannot measure and on which indeed we have only some very imprecise and general information. And because the effects of these facts in any particular instance cannot be confirmed by quantitative evidence, they are simply disregarded by those sworn to admit only what they regard as scientific evidence: they thereupon happily proceed on the fiction that the factors which they can measure are the only ones that are relevant.

The correlation between aggregate demand and total employment, for instance, may only be approximate, but as it is the *only* one on which we have quantitative data, it is accepted as the only causal connection that counts. On this standard there may thus well exist better "scientific" evidence for a false theory, which will be accepted because it is more "scientific," than for a valid explanation, which is rejected because there is no sufficient quantitative evidence for it.

Let me illustrate this by a brief sketch of what I regard as the chief actual cause of extensive unemployment—an account which will also explain why such unemployment cannot be lastingly cured by the inflationary policies recommended by the now fashionable theory. This correct explanation appears to me to be the existence of discrepancies between the distribution of demand among the different goods and services and the allocation of labor and other resources among the production of those outputs. We possess a fairly good "qualitative" knowledge of the forces by which a correspondence between demand and supply in the different sectors of the economic system is brought about, of the conditions under which it will be achieved, and of the factors likely to prevent such an adjustment. The separate steps in the account of this process rely on facts of everyday experience, and few who take the trouble to follow the argument will question the validity of the factual assumptions, or the logical correctness of the conclusions drawn from them. We have indeed good reason to believe that unemployment indicates that the structure of relative prices and wages has been distorted (usually by monopolistic or governmental price fixing), and that to restore equality between the demand and the supply of labor in all sectors changes of relative prices and some transfers of labor will be necessary.

But when we are asked for quantitative evidence for the particular structure of prices and wages that would be required in order to assure a smooth, continuous sale of the products and services offered, we must admit that we have no such information. We know, in other words, the general conditions in which what we call, somewhat misleadingly, an equilibrium will establish itself, but we never know what the particular prices or wages are which would exist if the market were to bring about such an equilibrium. We can merely say what the conditions are in which we can expect the market to establish prices and wages at which demand will equal supply. But we can never produce statistical information which would show how much the prevailing prices and wages *deviate* from those which would secure a continuous sale of the current supply of labor. Though this account of the causes of unemployment is an empirical theory, in the sense that it might be proved false, e.g. if, with a constant money supply, a general increase of wages did not lead to unemployment, it is certainly not the kind of theory which we could use to obtain specific numerical predictions concerning the rates of wages, or the distribution of labor, to be expected.

Why should we, however, in economics, have to plead ignorance of the sort of facts on which, in the case of a physical theory, a scientist would certainly be expected to give precise information? It is probably not surprising that those impressed by the example of the physical sciences should find this position very unsatisfactory and should insist on the standards of proof which they find there. The reason for this state of affairs is the fact, to which I have already briefly referred, that the social sciences, like much of biology but unlike most fields of the physical sciences, have to deal with structures of *essential* complexity, i.e. with structures whose characteristic properties can be exhibited only by models made up of relatively large numbers of variables. Competition, for instance, is a process which will produce certain results only if it proceeds among a fairly large number of acting persons.

In some fields, particularly where problems of a similar kind arise in the physical sciences, the difficulties can be overcome by using, instead of specific information about the individual elements, data about the relative frequency, or the probability, of the occurrence of the various distinctive properties of the elements. But this is true only where we have to deal with what has been called by Dr. Warren Weaver (formerly of the Rockefeller Foundation), with a distinction which ought to be much more widely understood, "phenomena of unorganized complexity," in contrast to those "phenomena of organized complexity" with which we have to deal in the social sciences.[2] Organized complexity here means that the character of the structures showing it depends not only on the properties of the individual elements of which they are composed, and the relative frequency with which they occur, but also on the manner in which the individual elements are connected with each other. In the explanation of the working of such structures we can for this reason not replace the information about the individual elements by statistical information, but require full information about each element if from our theory we are to derive specific predictions about individual events. Without such specific information about the individual elements we shall be confined to what on another occasion I have called mere pattern predictions—predictions of some of the general attributes of the structures that will form themselves, but not containing specific statements about the individual elements of which the structures will be made up.[3]

This is particularly true of our theories accounting for the determination of the systems of relative prices and wages that will form themselves on a well-functioning

---

2Warren Weaver, "A Quarter Century in the Natural Sciences," *The Rockefeller Foundation Annual Report 1958*, chapter I, "Science and Complexity."

3See my essay "The Theory of Complex Phenomena" in *The Critical Approach to Science and Philosophy. Essays in Honor of K. R. Popper*, ed. M. Bunge, New York 1964, and reprinted (with additions) in my *Studies in Philosophy, Politics and Economics*, London and Chicago 1967.

market. Into the determination of these prices and wages there will enter the effects of particular information possessed by every one of the participants in the market process—a sum of facts which in their totality cannot be known to the scientific observer, or to any other single brain. It is indeed the source of the superiority of the market order, and the reason why, when it is not suppressed by the powers of government, it regularly displaces other types of order, that in the resulting allocation of resources more of the knowledge of particular facts will be utilized which exists only dispersed among uncounted persons, than any one person can possess. But because we, the observing scientists, can thus never know all the determinants of such an order, and in consequence also cannot know at which particular structure of prices and wages demand would everywhere equal supply, we also cannot measure the deviations from that order; nor can we statistically test our theory that it is the deviations from that "equilibrium" system of prices and wages which make it impossible to sell some of the products and services at the prices at which they are offered.

Before I continue with my immediate concern, the effects of all this on the employment policies currently pursued, allow me to define more specifically the inherent limitations of our numerical knowledge which are so often overlooked. I want to do this to avoid giving the impression that I generally reject the mathematical method in economics. I regard it in fact as the great advantage of the mathematical technique that it allows us to describe, by means of algebraic equations, the general character of a pattern even where we are ignorant of the numerical values which will determine its particular manifestation. We could scarcely have achieved that comprehensive picture of the mutual interdependencies of the different events in a market without this algebraic technique. It has led to the illusion, however, that we can use this technique for the determination and prediction of the numerical values of those magnitudes; and this has led to a vain search for quantitative or numerical constants. This happened in spite of the fact that the modern founders of mathematical economics had no such illusions. It is true that their systems of equations describing the pattern of a market equilibrium are so framed that if we were able to fill in all the blanks of the abstract formulae, i.e. if we knew all the parameters of these equations, we could calculate the prices and quantities of all commodities and services sold. But, as Vilfredo Pareto, one of the founders of this theory, clearly stated, its purpose cannot be "to arrive at a numerical calculation of prices," because, as he said, it would be "absurd" to assume that we could ascertain all the data.[4] Indeed, the chief point was already seen by those remarkable anticipators of modern economics, the Spanish schoolmen of the sixteenth century, who emphasized that what they called *pretium mathematicum*, the mathematical price, depended on so many particular circumstances that it could never be known to man but was known only to God.[5] I sometimes wish that our mathematical economists would take this to heart. I must confess that I still doubt whether their search for measurable magnitudes has made significant contributions to our *theoretical* understanding of economic phenomena—as distinct from their value as a description of particular situations. Nor am I prepared to accept the excuse that this branch of research is still very young: Sir William Petty, the founder of econometrics, was after all a somewhat senior colleague of Sir Isaac Newton in the Royal Society!

---

[4]V. Pareto, *Manuel d'économie politique*, 2nd ed., Paris 1927, pp. 223–24.

[5]See, e.g., Luis Molina, *De iustitia et iure*, Cologne 1596–1600, tom. II, disp. 347, no. 3, and particularly Johannes de Lugo, *Disputationum de iustitia et iure tomus secundus*, Lyon 1642, disp. 26, sect. 4, no. 40.

There may be few instances in which the superstition that only measurable magnitudes can be important has done positive harm in the economic field: but the present inflation and employment problems are a very serious one. Its effect has been that what is probably the true cause of extensive unemployment has been disregarded by the scientistically minded majority of economists, because its operation could not be confirmed by directly observable relations between measurable magnitudes, and that an almost exclusive concentration on quantitatively measurable surface phenomena has produced a policy which has made matters worse.

It has, of course, to be readily admitted that the kind of theory which I regard as the true explanation of unemployment is a theory of somewhat limited content because it allows us to make only very general predictions of the *kind* of events which we must expect in a given situation. But the effects on policy of the more ambitious constructions have not been very fortunate and I confess that I prefer true but imperfect knowledge, even if it leaves much indetermined and unpredictable, to a pretense of exact knowledge that is likely to be false. The credit which the apparent conformity with recognized scientific standards can gain for seemingly simple but false theories may, as the present instance shows, have grave consequences.

In fact, in the case discussed, the very measures which the dominant "macro-economic" theory has recommended as a remedy for unemployment, namely the increase of aggregate demand, have become a cause of a very extensive misallocation of resources which is likely to make later large-scale unemployment inevitable. The continuous injection of additional amounts of money at points of the economic system where it creates a temporary demand which must cease when the increase of the quantity of money stops or slows down, together with the expectation of a continuing rise of prices, draws labor and other resources into employments which can last only so long as the increase of the quantity of money continues at the same rate—or perhaps even only so long as it continues to accelerate at a given rate. What this policy has produced is not so much a level of employment that could not have been brought about in other ways, as a distribution of employment which cannot be indefinitely maintained and which after some time can be maintained only by a rate of inflation which would rapidly lead to a disorganization of all economic activity. The fact is that by a mistaken theoretical view we have been led into a precarious position in which we cannot prevent substantial unemployment from re-appearing; not because, as this view is sometimes misrepresented, this unemployment is deliberately brought about as a means to combat inflation, but because it is now bound to occur as a deeply regrettable but inescapable consequence of the mistaken policies of the past as soon as inflation ceases to accelerate.

I must, however, now leave these problems of immediate practical importance which I have introduced chiefly as an illustration of the momentous consequences that may follow from errors concerning abstract problems of the philosophy of science. There is as much reason to be apprehensive about the long run dangers created in a much wider field by the uncritical acceptance of assertions which have the *appearance* of being scientific as there is with regard to the problems I have just discussed. What I mainly wanted to bring out by the topical illustration is that certainly in my field, but I believe also generally in the sciences of man, what looks superficially like the most scientific procedure is often the most unscientific, and, beyond this, that in these fields there are definite limits to what we can expect science to achieve. This means that to entrust to science—or to deliberate control according to scientific principles—more than the scientific method can achieve may have deplorable effects. The progress of the natural sciences in modern times has of course so much exceeded all expectations that any suggestion that there may be some limits to it is bound to arouse suspicion. Especially all those will resist such an insight who have hoped that our increasing power of prediction and control, generally regarded as the characteristic result of scientific advance, applied to the processes of society, would soon enable us to mold society entirely to our liking. It is indeed true that, in contrast to the exhilaration which the discoveries of the physical sciences tend to produce, the insights which we gain from the study of society more often have a dampening effect on our aspirations; and it is perhaps not surprising that the more impetuous younger members of our profession are not always prepared to accept this. Yet the confidence in the unlimited power of science is only too often based on a false belief that the scientific method consists in the application of a ready-made technique, or in imitating the form rather than the substance of scientific procedure, as if one needed only to follow some cooking recipes to solve all social problems. It sometimes almost seems as if the techniques of science were more easily learned than the thinking that shows us what the problems are and how to approach them.

The conflict between what in its present mood the public expects science to achieve in satisfaction of popular hopes and what is really in its power is a serious matter because, even if the true scientists should all recognize the limitations of what they can do in the field of human affairs, so long as the public expects more there will always be some who will pretend, and perhaps honestly believe, that they can do more to meet popular demands than is really in their power. It is often difficult enough for the expert, and certainly in many instances impossible for the layman, to distinguish between legitimate and illegitimate claims advanced in the name of science.

The enormous publicity recently given by the media to a report pronouncing in the name of science on *The Limits to Growth*, and the silence of the same media about the devastating criticism this report has received from the competent experts,[6] must make one feel somewhat apprehensive about the use to which the prestige of science can be put. But it is by no means only in the field of economics that far-reaching claims are made on behalf of a more scientific direction of all human activities and the desirability of replacing spontaneous processes by "conscious human control." If I am not mistaken, psychology, psychiatry, and some branches of sociology, not to speak about the so-called philosophy of history, are even more affected by what I have called the scientistic prejudice, and by specious claims of what science can achieve.[7]

If we are to safeguard the reputation of science, and to prevent the arrogation of knowledge based on a superficial similarity of procedure with that of the physical sciences, much effort will have to be directed toward debunking such arrogations, some of which have by now become the vested interests of established university departments. We cannot be grateful enough to such modern philosophers of science as Sir Karl Popper for giving us a test by which we can distinguish between what we may accept as scien-

---

[6]See *The Limits to Growth: A Report of the Club of Rome's Project on the Predicament of Mankind*, New York 1972; for a systematic examination of this by a competent economist cf. Wilfred Beckerman, *In Defence of Economic Growth*, London 1974, and, for a list of earlier criticisms by experts, Gottfried Haberler, *Economic Growth and Stability*, Los Angeles 1974, who rightly calls their effect "devastating."

[7]I have given some illustrations of these tendencies in other fields in my inaugural lecture as Visiting Professor at the University of Salzburg, *Die Irrtümer des Konstruktivismus und die Grundlagen legitimer Kritik gesellschaftlicher Gebilde*, Munich 1970, now reissued for the Walter Eucken Institute at Freiburg i.Brg. by J. C. B. Mohr, Tübingen 1975.

tific and what not—a test which I am sure some doctrines now widely accepted as scientific would not pass. There are some special problems, however, in connection with those essentially complex phenomena of which social structures are so important an instance, which make me wish to restate in conclusion in more general terms the reasons why in these fields not only are there absolute obstacles to the prediction of specific events, but to act as if we possessed scientific knowledge enabling us to transcend them may itself become a serious obstacle to the advance of the human intellect.

The chief point we must remember is that the great and rapid advance of the physical sciences took place in fields where it proved that explanation and prediction could be based on laws which accounted for the observed phenomena as functions of comparatively few variables—either particular facts or relative frequencies of events. This may even be the ultimate reason why we single out these realms as "physical" in contrast to those more highly organized structures which I have here called essentially complex phenomena. There is no reason why the position must be the same in the latter as in the former fields. The difficulties which we encounter in the latter are not, as one might at first suspect, difficulties about formulating theories for the explanation of the observed events—although they cause also special difficulties about testing proposed explanations and therefore about eliminating bad theories. They are due to the chief problem which arises when we apply our theories to any particular situation in the real world. A theory of essentially complex phenomena must refer to a large number of particular facts; and to derive a prediction from it, or to test it, we have to ascertain all these particular facts. Once we have succeeded in this there should be no particular difficulty about deriving testable predictions—with the help of modern computers it should be easy enough to insert these data into the appropriate blanks of the theoretical formulae and to derive a prediction. The real difficulty, to the solution of which science has little to contribute, and which is sometimes indeed insoluble, consists in the ascertainment of the particular facts.

A simple example will show the nature of this difficulty. Consider some ball game played by a few people of approximately equal skill. If we knew a few particular facts in addition to our general knowledge of the ability of the individual players, such as their state of attention, their perceptions, and the state of their hearts, lungs, muscles, etc. at each moment of the game, we could probably predict the outcome. Indeed, if we were familiar both with the game and the teams we should probably have a fairly shrewd idea on what the outcome will depend. But we shall of course not be able to ascertain those facts and in consequence the result of the game will be outside the range of the scientifically predictable, however well we may know what effects particular events would have on the result of the game. This does not mean that we can make no predictions at all about the course of such a game. If we know the rules of the different games we shall, in watching one, very soon know which game is being played and what kinds of actions we can expect and what kind not. But our capacity to predict will be confined to such general characteristics of the events to be expected and not include the capacity of predicting particular individual events.

This corresponds to what I have called earlier the mere pattern predictions to which we are increasingly confined as we penetrate from the realm in which relatively simple laws prevail into the range of phenomena where organized complexity rules. As we advance we find more and more frequently that we can in fact ascertain only some but not all the particular circumstances which determine the outcome of a given process; and in consequence we are able to predict only some but not all the properties of the result we have to expect. Often all that we shall be able to predict will be some abstract characteristic of the pattern that will appear—relations between kinds of elements about which individually we know very little. Yet, as I am anxious to repeat, we will still achieve predictions which can be falsified and which therefore are of empirical significance.

Of course, compared with the precise predictions we have learned to expect in the physical sciences, this sort of mere pattern predictions is a second best with which one does not like to have to be content. Yet the danger of which I want to warn is precisely the belief that in order to have a claim to be accepted as scientific it is necessary to achieve more. This way lies charlatanism and worse. To act on the belief that we possess the knowledge and the power which enable us to shape the processes of society entirely to our liking, knowledge which in fact we do *not* possess, is likely to make us do much harm. In the physical sciences there may be little objection to trying to do the impossible; one might even feel that one ought not to discourage the over-confident because their experiments may after all produce some new insights. But in the social field the erroneous belief that the exercise of some power would have beneficial consequences is likely to lead to a new power to coerce other men being conferred on some authority. Even if such power is not in itself bad, its exercise is likely to impede the functioning of those spontaneous ordering forces by which, without understanding them, man is in fact so largely assisted in the pursuit of his aims. We are only beginning to understand on how subtle a communication system the functioning of an advanced industrial society is based—a communications system which we call the market and which turns out to be a more efficient mechanism for digesting dispersed information than any that man has deliberately designed.

If man is not to do more harm than good in his efforts to improve the social order, he will have to learn that in this, as in all other fields where essential complexity of an organized kind prevails, he cannot acquire the full knowledge which would make mastery of the events possible. He will therefore have to use what knowledge he can achieve, not to shape the results as the craftsman shapes his handiwork, but rather to cultivate a growth by providing the appropriate environment, in the manner in which the gardener does this for his plants. There is danger in the exuberant feeling of ever growing power which the advance of the physical sciences has engendered and which tempts man to try, "dizzy with success," to use a characteristic phrase of early communism, to subject not only our natural but also our human environment to the control of a human will. The recognition of the insuperable limits to his knowledge ought indeed to teach the student of society a lesson of humility which should guard him against becoming an accomplice in men's fatal striving to control society—a striving which makes him not only a tyrant over his fellows, but which may well make him the destroyer of a civilization which no brain has designed but which has grown from the free efforts of millions of individuals.

Chapter 7

Choice in Currency: A Way to Stop Inflation*

I

Money, Keynes, and History

The chief root of our present monetary troubles is, of course, the sanction of scientific authority which Lord Keynes and his disciples have given to the age-old superstition that by increasing the aggregate of money expenditure we can lastingly ensure prosperity and full employment. It is a superstition against which economists before Keynes had struggled with some success for at least two centuries. It had governed most of earlier history. This history, indeed, has been largely a history of inflation; significantly, it was only during the rise of the prosperous modern industrial systems and during the rule of the gold standard that over a period of about two hundred years (in Britain from about 1714 to 1914, and in the United States from about 1749 to 1939) prices were at the end about where they had been at the beginning. During this unique period of monetary stability the gold standard had imposed upon monetary authorities a discipline which

*This text is based on the Institute of Economic Affairs' 2007 web edition of this essay, which is based on Hayek's address "International Money," delivered to the Geneva Gold and Monetary Conference on September 25, 1975, in Lausanne, Switzerland.

prevented them from abusing their powers, as they have done at nearly all other times. Experience in other parts of the world does not seem to have been very different: I have been told that a Chinese law attempted to prohibit paper money for all times (of course, ineffectively), long before the Europeans ever invented it!

Keynesian Rehabilitation

It was John Maynard Keynes, a man of great intellect but limited knowledge of economic theory, who ultimately succeeded in rehabilitating a view long the preserve of cranks with whom he openly sympathized. He had attempted by a succession of new theories to justify the same superficially persuasive, intuitive belief that had been held by many practical men before, but that will not withstand rigorous analysis of the price mechanism: just as there cannot be a uniform price for all kinds of labor, an equality of demand and supply for labor in general cannot be secured by managing *aggregate* demand. The volume of employment depends on the correspondence of demand and supply *in each sector* of the economy, and therefore on the wage structure and the distribution of demand between the sectors. The consequence is that over a longer period the Keynesian remedy does not cure unemployment but makes it worse.

The claim of an eminent public figure and brilliant polemicist to provide a cheap and easy means of permanently preventing serious unemployment conquered public opinion and, after his death, professional opinion too. Sir John Hicks has even proposed that we call the third quarter of this century, 1950 to 1975, the age of Keynes, as the second quarter was the age of Hitler.[1] I do not feel that

---

[1]John Hicks, *The Crisis in Keynesian Economics*, Oxford University Press, 1974, p. 1.

the harm Keynes did is really so much as to justify *that* description. But it is true that, so long as his prescriptions seemed to work, they operated as an orthodoxy which it appeared useless to oppose.

Personal Confession

I have often blamed myself for having given up the struggle after I had spent much time and energy criticizing the first version of Keynes's theoretical framework. Only after the second part of my critique had appeared did he tell me he had changed his mind and no longer believed what he had said in the *Treatise on Money* of 1930 (somewhat unjustly towards himself, as it seems to me, since I still believe that volume II of the *Treatise* contains some of the best work he ever did). At any rate, I felt it then to be useless to return to the charge, because he seemed so likely to change his views again. When it proved that this new version—the *General Theory* of 1936—conquered most of the professional opinion, and when in the end even some of the colleagues I most respected supported the wholly Keynesian Bretton Woods agreement, I largely withdrew from the debate, since to proclaim my dissent from the near-unanimous views of the orthodox phalanx would merely have deprived me of a hearing on other matters about which I was more concerned at the time. (I believe, however, that, so far as some of the best British economists were concerned, their support of Bretton Woods was determined more by a misguided patriotism—the hope that it would benefit Britain in her postwar difficulties—than by a belief that it would provide a satisfactory international monetary order.)

II

The Manufacture of Unemployment

I wrote 36 years ago on the crucial point of difference:

> It may perhaps be pointed out that it has, of course, never been denied that employment can be rapidly increased, and a position of "full employment" achieved in the shortest possible time, by means of monetary expansion—least of all by those economists whose outlook has been influenced by the experience of a major inflation. All that has been contended is that the kind of full employment which can be created in this way is inherently unstable, and that to create employment by these means is to perpetuate fluctuations. There may be desperate situations in which it may indeed be necessary to increase employment at all costs, even if it be only for a short period—perhaps the situation in which Dr. Brüning found himself in Germany in 1932 was such a situation in which desperate means would have been justified. But the economist should not conceal the fact that to aim at the maximum of employment which can be achieved in the short run by means of monetary policy is essentially the policy of the desperado who has nothing to lose and everything to gain from a short breathing space.[2]

To this I would now like to add, in reply to the constant deliberate misrepresentation of my views by politicians, who like to picture me as a sort of bogey whose influence makes conservative parties dangerous, what I

---

[2]F. A. Hayek, *Profits, Interest and Investment*, Routledge & Kegan Paul, London, 1939, p. 63n.

regularly emphasize and stated nine months ago in my Nobel Memorial Prize Lecture at Stockholm in the following words:

> The truth is that by a mistaken theoretical view we have been led into a precarious position in which we cannot prevent substantial unemployment from re-appearing: not because, as my view is sometimes misrepresented, this unemployment is deliberately brought about as a means to combat inflation, but because it is now bound to appear as a deeply regrettable but *inescapable* consequence of the mistaken policies of the past as soon as inflation ceases to accelerate.[3]

Unemployment via "Full Employment Policies"

This manufacture of unemployment by what are called "full employment policies" is a complex process. In essence it operates by temporary changes in the distribution of demand, drawing both unemployed and already employed workers into jobs which will disappear with the end of inflation. In the periodically recurrent crises of the pre-1914 years the expansion of credit during the preceding boom served largely to finance industrial investment, and the over-development and subsequent unemployment occurred mainly in the industries producing capital equipment. In the engineered inflation of the last decades things were more complex.

What will happen during a major inflation is illustrated by an observation from the early 1920s which many of my Viennese contemporaries will confirm: in the city many of the famous coffee houses were driven from the

[3] F. A. Hayek, "The Pretence of Knowledge," Nobel Memorial Prize Lecture 1974, reprinted in *Full Employment at Any Price?*, Occasional Paper 45, IEA, 1975, p. 37.

best corner sites by new bank offices and returned after the "stabilization crisis," when the banks had contracted or collapsed and thousands of bank clerks swelled the ranks of the unemployed.

The Lost Generation

The whole theory underlying the full employment policies has by now of course been thoroughly discredited by the experience of the last few years. In consequence the economists are also beginning to discover its fatal intellectual defects, which they ought to have seen all along. Yet I fear the theory will still give us a lot of trouble: it has left us with a lost generation of economists who have learned nothing else. One of our chief problems will be to protect our money against those economists who will continue to offer their quack remedies, the short-term effectiveness of which will continue to ensure them popularity. It will survive among blind doctrinaires who have always been convinced that they have the key to salvation.

The 1863 Penny

In consequence, though the rapid descent of Keynesian doctrine from intellectual respectability can be denied no longer, it still gravely threatens the chances of a sensible monetary policy. Nor have people yet fully realized how much irreparable damage it has already done, particularly in Britain, the country of its origin. The sense of financial respectability which once guided British monetary policy has rapidly disappeared. From a model to be imitated Britain has in a few years descended to be a warning example for the rest of the world. This decay was recently brought home to me by a curious incident: I found in a drawer of my desk a British penny dated 1863 which a short 12 years ago, that is, when it was exactly a hundred years old, I had received as change from a London bus conductor and had taken back to Germany to show to my students what long-run monetary stability meant. I believe they were duly impressed. But they would laugh in my face if I now mentioned Britain as an instance of monetary stability.

III

The Weakness of Political Control of Money

A wise man should perhaps have foreseen that less than 30 years after the nationalization of the Bank of England the purchasing power of the pound sterling would have been reduced to less than one-quarter of what it had been at that date. As has sooner or later happened everywhere, government control of the quantity of money has once again proved fatal. I do not want to question that a very intelligent and wholly independent national or international monetary authority *might* do better than an international gold standard, or any other sort of automatic system. But I see not the slightest hope that any government, or any institution subject to political pressure, will ever be able to act in such a manner.

Group Interests Harmful

I never had much illusion in this respect, but I must confess that in the course of a long life my opinion of governments has steadily worsened: the more intelligently they try to act (as distinguished from simply following an established rule), the more harm they seem to do—because once they are known to aim at particular goals (rather than merely maintaining a self-correcting spontaneous order) the less they can avoid serving sectional interests. And the demands of all organized group interests are almost invariably harmful—except only when they protest against restrictions imposed upon them for the benefit of other group interests. I am by no means re-assured by the fact that, at least in some countries, the civil servants who run affairs are mostly intelligent, well-meaning, and honest men. The point is that, if governments are to remain in office in the prevailing political order, they have no choice but to use their powers for the benefit of particular groups—and one strong interest is always to get additional money for extra expenditure. However harmful inflation is in general seen to be, there are always substantial groups of people, including some for whose support collectivist-inclined governments primarily look, which in the short run greatly gain by it—even if only by staving off for some time the loss of an income which it is human nature to believe will be only temporary if they can tide over the emergency.

Rebuilding the Resistances to Inflation

The pressure for more and cheaper money is an ever-present political force which monetary authorities have never been able to resist, unless they were in a position credibly to point to an absolute obstacle which made it impossible for them to meet such demands. And it will become even more irresistible when these interests can appeal to an increasingly unrecognizable image of St. Maynard. There will be no more urgent need than to erect new defenses against the onslaughts of popular forms of Keynesianism, that is, to replace or restore those restraints which, under the influence of his theory, have been systematically dismantled. It was the main function of the gold standard, of balanced budgets, of the necessity for deficit countries to contract their circulation, and of the limitation of the supply of "international liquidity," to make it impossible for the monetary authorities to capitulate to the pressure for more money. And it was exactly for that reason that all these safeguards against inflation, which had made it possible for representative governments to resist the demands of powerful pressure groups for more money, have been removed at the instigation of economists who imagined that, if governments were released from the shackles of mechanical rules, they would be able to act wisely for the general benefit.

I do not believe we can now remedy this position by *constructing* some new international monetary order, whether a new international monetary authority or institution, or even an international agreement to adopt a particular mechanism or system of policy, such as the classical gold standard. I am fairly convinced that any attempt now to re-instate the gold standard by international agreement would break down within a short time and merely discredit the ideal of an international gold standard for even longer. Without the conviction of the public at large that certain immediately painful measures are occasionally necessary to preserve reasonable stability, we cannot hope that any authority which has power to determine the quantity of money will long resist the pressure for, or the seduction of, cheap money.

Protecting Money from Politics

The politician, acting on a modified Keynesian maxim that in the long run we are all out of office, does not care if his successful cure of unemployment is bound to produce more unemployment in the future. The politicians who will be blamed for it will not be those who created the inflation but those who stopped it. No worse trap could have been set for a democratic system in which the government is forced to act on the beliefs that the people think to be true. Our only hope for a stable money is indeed now to find a way to protect money from politics.

With the exception only of the 200-year period of the gold standard, practically all governments of history have used their exclusive power to issue money in order to defraud and plunder the people. There is less ground than ever for hoping that, so long as the people have no choice but to use the money their government provides, governments will become more trustworthy. Under the prevailing systems of government, which are supposed to be guided by the opinion of the majority but under which in practice any sizeable group may create a "political necessity" for the government by threatening to withhold the votes it needs to claim majority support, we cannot entrust dangerous instruments to it. Fortunately we need not yet fear, I hope, that governments will start a war to please some indispensable group of supporters, but money is certainly too dangerous an instrument to leave to the fortuitous expediency of politicians—or, it seems, economists.

A Dangerous Monopoly

What is so dangerous and ought to be done away with is not governments' right to issue money but the *exclusive* right to do so and their power to force people to use it and to accept it at a particular price. This monopoly of government, like the postal monopoly, has its origin not in any benefit it secures for the people but solely in the desire to enhance the coercive powers of government. I doubt whether it has ever done any good except to the rulers and their favorites. All history contradicts the belief that governments have given us a safer money than we would have had without their claiming an exclusive right to issue it.

IV

Choice of Money for Payment in Contracts

But why should we not let people choose freely what money they want to use? By "people" I mean the individuals who ought to have the right to decide whether they want to buy or sell for francs, pounds, dollars, D-marks, or ounces of gold. I have no objection to governments issuing money, but I believe their claim to a *monopoly*, or their power to *limit* the kinds of money in which contracts may be concluded within their territory, or to determine the *rates* at which monies can be exchanged, to be wholly harmful.

At this moment it seems that the best thing we could wish governments to do is for, say, all the members of the European Economic Community, or, better still, all the governments of the Atlantic Community, to bind themselves mutually not to place any restrictions on the free use within their territories of one another's—or any other—currencies, including their purchase and sale at any price the parties decide upon, or on their use as accounting units in which to keep books. This, and not a utopian European Monetary Unit, seems to me now both the practicable and the desirable arrangement to aim at. To make the scheme effective it would be important, for reasons I state later, also to provide that banks in one country be free to establish branches in any of the others.

Government and Legal Tender

This suggestion may at first seem absurd to all brought up on the concept of "legal tender." Is it not essential that the law designate one kind of money as the legal money? This is, however, true only to the extent that, *if* the government does issue money, it must also say what must be accepted in discharge of debts incurred in that money. And it must also determine in what manner certain noncontractual legal obligations, such as taxes or liabilities for damage or torts, are to be discharged. But there is no reason whatever why people should not be free to make contracts, including ordinary purchases and sales, in any kind of money they choose, or why they should be obliged to sell against any particular kind of money.

There could be no more effective check against the abuse of money by the government than if people were free to refuse any money they distrusted and to prefer money in which they had confidence. Nor could there be a stronger inducement to governments to ensure the stability of their money than the knowledge that, so long as they kept the supply below the demand for it, that demand would tend to grow. Therefore, let us deprive governments (or their monetary authorities) of all power to protect their money against competition: if they can no longer conceal that their money is becoming bad, they will have to restrict the issue.

The first reaction of many readers may be to ask whether the effect of such a system would not according to an old rule be that the bad money would drive out the good. But this would be a misunderstanding of what is called Gresham's Law. This indeed is one of the oldest insights into the mechanism of money, so old that 2,400 years ago Aristophanes, in one of his comedies, could say that it was with politicians as it is with coins, because the bad ones drive out the good.[4] But the truth which apparently even today is not generally understood is that Gresham's Law operates *only* if the two kinds of money

---

[4]Aristophanes, *Frogs*, 891–98, in Frere's translation:

Oftentimes we have reflected on a similar abuse
In the choice of men for office, and of coins for common use,
For our old and standard pieces, valued and approved and tried,
Here among the Grecian nations, and in all the world besides,
Recognized in every realm for trusty stamp and pure assay,
Are rejected and abandoned for the trash of yesterday,
For a vile adulterated issue, drossy, counterfeit and base,
Which the traffic of the city passes current in their place.

About the same time, the philosopher Diogenes called money "the legislators' game of dice"!

have to be accepted at a prescribed rate of exchange. Exactly the opposite will happen when people are free to exchange the different kinds of money at whatever rate they can agree upon. This was observed many times during the great inflations when even the most severe penalties threatened by governments could not prevent people from using other kinds of money—even commodities like cigarettes and bottles of brandy rather than the government money—which clearly meant that the good money was driving out the bad.[5]

Benefits of Free Currency System

Make it merely legal and people will be very quick indeed to refuse to use the national currency once it depreciates noticeably, and they will make their dealings in a currency they trust. Employers, in particular, would find it in their interest to offer, in collective agreements, not wages anticipating a foreseen rise of prices but wages in a currency they trusted and could make the basis of rational calculation. This would deprive government of the power to counteract excessive wage increases, and the unemployment they would cause, by depreciating their currency. It would also prevent employers from conceding such wages in the expectation that the national monetary authority would bail them out if they promised more than they could pay.

There is no reason to be concerned about the effects of such an arrangement on ordinary men who know neither how to handle nor how to obtain strange kinds of money. So long as the shopkeepers knew that they could turn it

---

[5]During the German inflation after the First World War, when people began to use dollars and other solid currencies in the place of marks, a Dutch financier (if I rightly remember, Mr. Vissering) asserted that Gresham's Law was false and the opposite is true.

instantly at the current rate of exchange into whatever money they preferred, they would be *only* too ready to sell their wares at an appropriate price for any currency. But the malpractices of government would show themselves much more rapidly if prices rose *only* in terms of the money issued by it, and people would soon learn to hold the government responsible for the value of the money in which they were paid. Electronic calculators, which in seconds would give the equivalent of any price in any currency at the current rate, would soon be used everywhere. But, unless the national government all too badly mismanaged the currency it issued, it would probably be continued to be used in everyday retail transactions. What would be affected mostly would be not so much the use of money in daily payments as the willingness to *hold* different kinds of money. It would mainly be the tendency of all business and capital transactions rapidly to switch to a more reliable standard (and to base calculations and accounting on it) which would keep national monetary policy on the right path.

V

Long-Run Monetary Stability

The upshot would probably be that the currencies of those countries trusted to pursue a responsible monetary policy would tend to displace gradually those of a less reliable character. The reputation of financial righteousness would become a jealously guarded asset of all issuers of money, since they would know that even the slightest deviation from the path of honesty would reduce the demand for their product.

I do not believe there is any reason to fear that in such a competition for the most general acceptance of a currency there would arise a tendency to deflation or an increasing value of money. People will be quite as reluctant to borrow or incur debts in a currency expected to appreciate as they will hesitate to lend in a currency expected to depreciate. The convenience of use is decidedly in favor of a currency which can be expected to retain an approximately stable value. If governments and other issuers of money have to compete in inducing people to *hold* their money, and make long-term contracts in it, they will have to create confidence in its long-run stability.

"The Universal Prize"

Where I am not sure is whether in such a competition for reliability any government-issued currency would prevail, or whether the predominant preference would not be in favor of some such units as ounces of gold. It seems not unlikely that gold would ultimately re-assert its place as "the universal prize in all countries, in all cultures, in all ages," as Jacob Bronowski has recently called it in his brilliant book on *The Ascent of Man*,[6] if people were given complete freedom to decide what to use as their standard and general medium of exchange—more likely, at any rate, than as the result of any organized attempt to restore the gold standard.

The reason why, in order to be fully effective, the free international market in currencies should extend also to the services of banks is, of course, that bank deposits subject to check represent today much the largest part of the liquid assets of most people. Even during the last hundred years or so of the gold standard this circumstance increasingly prevented it from operating as a fully international currency, because any inflow or outflow in or out of a country required a proportionate expansion or contraction of the much larger super-structure of the

---

[6]Jacob Bronowski, *The Ascent of Man*, BBC Publications, London, 1973.

national credit money, the effect of which falls indiscriminately on the whole economy instead of merely increasing or decreasing the demand for the particular goods which was required to bring about a new balance between imports and exports. With a truly international banking system money could be transferred directly without producing the harmful process of secondary contractions or expansions of the credit structure.

It would probably also impose the most effective discipline on governments if they felt immediately the effects of their policies on the attractiveness of investment in their country. I have *just* read in an English Whig tract more than 250 years old: "Who would establish a Bank in an arbitrary country, or trust his money constantly there?"[7] The tract, incidentally, tells us that yet another 50 years earlier a great French banker, Jean-Baptiste Tavernier, invested all the riches he had amassed in his long rambles over the world in what the authors described as "the barren rocks of Switzerland"; when asked why by Louis XIV, he had the courage to tell him that "he was willing to have something which he could call his own!" Switzerland, apparently, laid the foundations of her prosperity earlier than most people realize.

Free Dealings in Money Better than Monetary Unions

I prefer the freeing of all dealings in money to any sort of monetary union also because the latter would demand an international monetary authority which I believe is neither practicable nor even desirable—and hardly to be more trusted than a national authority. It seems to me that there is a very sound element in the

---

[7]Thomas Gordon and John Trenchard, *The Cato Letters*, letters dated 12 May, 1722, and 3 February, 1721, respectively, published in collected editions, London, 1724, and later.

widespread disinclination to confer sovereign powers, or at least powers to command, on any international authority. What we need are not international authorities possessing powers of direction, but merely international bodies (or, rather, international treaties which are effectively enforced) which can prohibit certain actions of governments that will harm other people. Effectively to prohibit all restrictions on dealings in (and the possession of) different kinds of money (or claims for money) would at last make it possible that the absence of tariffs, or other obstacles to the movement of goods and men, will secure a genuine free trade area or common market—and do more than anything else to create confidence in the countries committing themselves to it. It is now urgently needed to counter that monetary nationalism that I first criticized almost 40 years ago[8] and which is becoming even more dangerous when, as a consequence of the close kinship between the two views, it is turning into monetary socialism. I hope it will not be too long before complete freedom to deal in any money one likes will be regarded as the essential mark of a free country.[9]

You may feel that my proposal amounts to no less than the abolition of monetary policy; and you would not be quite wrong. As in other connections, I have come to the conclusion that the best the state can do with respect

---

8 *Monetary Nationalism and International Stability*, Longmans, London, 1937.

9 It may at first seem as if this suggestion were in conflict with my general support of fixed exchange rates under the present system. But this is not so. Fixed exchange rates seem to me to be necessary so long as national governments have a monopoly of issuing money in their territory in order to place them under a very necessary discipline. But this is of course no longer necessary when they have to submit to the discipline of competition with other issuers of money equally current within their territory.

to money is to provide a framework of legal rules within which the people can develop the monetary institutions that best suit them. It seems to me that if we could prevent governments from meddling with money, we would do more good than any government has ever done in this regard. And private enterprise would probably have done better than the best they have ever done.

Annotated Bibliography

Prepared by David Gordon

The items included are listed, for the most part, by the date of publication of the first English edition. In my comments on Hayek's books about monetary theory and the business cycle, I have relied on Joseph T. Salerno's introduction to *Prices and Production and Other Works*, Ludwig von Mises Institute 2008.

Prices and Production. New York: Macmillan, 1932. A full statement of Austrian business cycle theory. It stresses how money influences the stages of production.

Monetary Theory and the Trade Cycle. London: Jonathan Cape, 1933. Refutes naïve advocates of the quantity theory of money, who assume a fixed relationship between the quantity of money and the price level, neglecting the effects of monetary expansion on the stages of production. Irving Fisher and Gustav Cassel are among the economists criticized.

Monetary Nationalism and International Stability. London: Longmans, Green, 1937. Analyzes the international operation of the pure gold standard. Hayek is very critical of the influence of "monetary nationalism" after World War I. The monetary nationalists favored price stability through monetary policy, with freely fluctuating exchange rates. Hayek opposes these policies.

The Pure Theory of Capital. Chicago: University of Chicago Press, 1941. Discusses capital and intertemporal interest rates. The heterogeneity of capital and its relation to the passage of time is an important theme. This is one of Hayek's most difficult books.

The Road to Serfdom. London: George Routledge & Sons, 1944. Argues that economic planning leads to the suppression of freedom. A centrally planned economy is inconsistent with the rule of law. "Why the Worst Get on Top" is a famous chapter. This is Hayek's most popular book.

Individualism and Economic Order. Chicago: University of Chicago Press, 1948. An essay collection that includes "The Meaning of Competition" and "Free Enterprise and Competitive Order." These two essays argue that the abstractions of equilibrium analysis should not be a guide to economic policy. Other essays discuss Hayek's contribution to the debate on the socialist calculation argument. Hayek's criticism of Oscar Lange's "competitive solution" is especially noteworthy.

John Stuart Mill and Harriet Taylor: Their Friendship and Subsequent Marriage. Chicago: University of Chicago Press, 1951. A dual biography that traces the stages in the relationship between Mill and Taylor. Hayek contends that Taylor made Mill more of a rigorous rationalist than before he came under her influence, to his detriment.

The Counter-Revolution of Science: Studies on the Abuse of Reason. Glencoe, IL: The Free Press, 1952. Social planning reflects an engineering mentality, in contrast to the subjectivist method which is proper to the social sciences. The influence of Saint-Simon and his quondam disciple and later rival Comte is stressed. Includes a comparison of Comte and Hegel.

The Sensory Order: An Inquiry into the Foundations of Theoretical Psychology. Chicago: University of Chicago Press, 1952. The mind operates through structures of classification, most of which are inaccessible to our consciousness. Strongly critical of behaviorism.

The Constitution of Liberty. Chicago: University of Chicago Press, 1960. A detailed history of the development of freedom and the rule of law, emphasizing the contributions of English thinkers. Hayek sketches the institutional framework he believes is appropriate for a free society.

Studies in Philosophy, Politics and Economics. Chicago: University of Chicago Press, 1967. A number of the essays in this collection discuss spontaneous order. The collection includes "The Non Sequitur of the 'Dependence Effect,'" which criticizes J. K. Galbraith's charge that business uses advertising to induce artificial demand. "The Intellectuals and Socialism" argues that the "second-hand dealers in ideas" have a propensity to abstract thinking, making them unappreciative of the undirected way in which the free market works,

Law, Legislation and Liberty. Vol. 1, *Rules and Order*. Chicago: University of Chicago Press, 1973. Stresses the value of a liberal, spontaneous order as opposed to an engineered order. Legislation should be confined to general rules, and the common law, as opposed to legislated law, was a key factor in the development of a free society.

—. Vol. 2, *The Mirage of Social Justice*. Chicago: University of Chicago Press, 1976. Argues that the concept of "social justice" can only arise for a planned economic order. There are no sperate principles of distribution in the free market, and its outcomes are neither "fair" nor "unfair".

—. Vol. 3, *The Political Order of a Free People*. Chicago, University of Chicago Press, 1979. Strongly critical of unrestricted majority-rule democracy, arguing that this is inconsistent with the rule of law. The legislature should be confined to enacting general rules.

New Studies in Philosophy, Politics, Economics and the History of Ideas. Chicago: University of Chicago Press, 1978. Includes "Competition as a Discovery Procedure" and Hayek's Nobel Prize speech, "The Pretence of Knowledge," arguing that economists cannot properly make predictions about the effects of particular policies based on abstract models, because these models only allow "pattern prediction."

The Denationalisation of Money: The Argument Refined. London: Institute for Economic Affairs, 1980. Calls for competition among private issuers of currency and suggests that this would lead to convergence on a common standard.

The Fatal Conceit: The Errors of Socialism. Vol. 1 of *The Collected Works of F. A. Hayek*. Chicago: University of Chicago Press, 1991. A posthumous publication, edited by W. W. Bartley III. Argues against "constructivist rationalism" and suggests that socialism is a revival of animistic thought. The book is sympathetic to the role of religion and tradition and critical of psychoanalysis for its negative impact on the family.

Index

Compiled by Roger E. Bissell